Benghazi:

The Complete Inside Report on the Terrorist Attacks

Providence Research Publishing

Foreward

On the evening of September 11, 2012, Islamic militants attacked the American diplomatic compound in Benghazi, Libya, killingU.S. Ambassador J. Christopher Stevens and U.S. Foreign Service Information Management Officer Sean Smith. Stevens was the first U.S. Ambassador killed on duty since 1979.

Several hours later, a second assault targeted a different compound about one mile away, killing two CIA contractors, Tyrone S. Woods and Glen Doherty. Ten others were also injured in the attacks.

Many Libyans condemned the attacks and praised the late ambassador. They staged public demonstrations condemning the militias (formed during the civil war to oppose leader Colonel Muammar Gaddafi), which were suspected of the attacks.

The United States immediately increased security worldwide at diplomatic and military facilities and began investigating the Benghazi attack. In the aftermath of the attack, State Department officials were criticized for denying requests for additional security at the consulate prior to the attack. As Secretary of State, Hillary Clinton subsequently took responsibility for the security lapses.

Initially, it was reported by the media the Benghazi attack was a spontaneous protest triggered by an anti-Muslim video, Innocence of Muslims. Subsequent investigations determined that there was no such protest and that the attacks were premeditated, though captured suspect Ahmed Abu Khattala stated that the assault was in retaliation for the video.

On August 6, 2013, it was reported that the U.S. had filed criminal charges against several individuals, including militia leaderAhmed Abu Khattala, for alleged involvement in the attacks. Khattala has been described by Libyan and U.S. officials as the Benghazi leader of Ansar al-Sharia, which was listed in January 2014 by the U.S. Department of State as a terror organization. On the weekend of June 14, 2014, U.S. special forces, in coordination with the FBI, captured Khattala in Libya.

Timeline of the Attacks

9:40 p.m.: Gunfire is heard outside the Benghazi diplomatic mission, then a loud explosion. Dozens of armed militiamen charge the main gate and set fire to a barracks building as they make for the ambassador's residence.

10 p.m.: Attackers breach the mission walls and make for the ambassador's residence. Stevens and information officer Sean Smith run to a safe room with one security agent.
An alert is sent to the CIA security team at an annex about a mile away, the State Department and the U.S. Embassy in Tripoli. Stevens calls deputy mission chief Gregory Hicks at the embassy and tells him, "Greg, we're under attack."

10:30 p.m.: Stevens and Smith have taken refuge behind a fortified door with heavy metal bars that keeps the attackers from breaking in, but they set fire to the villa with diesel fuel. Within minutes, Stevens and Smith are overwhelmed by smoke.
At about the same time, six U.S. security agents leave the CIA annex for the main building. They and 16 Libyan security guards regain control over the compound and start searching for Stevens and Smith.

Shortly after 11 p.m.: A U.S. surveillance drone arrives over Benghazi. Then-Defense Secretary Leon Panetta and Joint Chiefs Chairman Martin Dempsey meet with President Barack Obama.

12:07 a.m., September 12: The State Department sends an e-mail to the White House, the Pentagon and the FBI indicating the Islamic militant group Ansar al-Sharia claimed credit for the attack.

1:15 a.m.: A rescue team from Tripoli arrives in Benghazi. About 30 Americans have been rescued from the consulate building and are holed up with the Stevens at the CIA annex.

2 a.m.: Hicks informs Secretary of State Hillary Clinton that they need to evacuate all Americans from Benghazi. At about the same time, an eyewitness captures on video Stevens being pulled from the smoke-filled building.

4 a.m.: The attackers launch a full-on assault against the annex, dropping mortars on the roof. Navy SEALs Glen Doherty and Tyrone Woods are killed in the attack.

10 a.m.: The bodies of Stevens, Smith, Doherty and Woods are put on the last plane out of Benghazi.

Background

Islamic militancy in the Libyan Civil War

Militants like Abdul Hakeem Belhaj, who fought alongside Al-Qaeda in Afghanistan, other former members of the Libyan Islamic Fighting Group or other radical movements, as well as jihadists who had fought in Iraq and Afghanistan were essential in the effort to overthrow Gadhafi. That spring, weapons began being shipped to rebels through Qatar with American approval. By September 2011, Western counterterrorism officials had become increasingly concerned with the role Islamic radicals were playing in the revolt in Libya, and worried the weapons acquired by them during the war would be used in future terrorist attacks.

American presence in Libya and Benghazi

Within months of the start of the Libyan revolution in February 2011, the CIA began building a meaningful but covert presence in Benghazi. During the war, elite counter-terrorist operators from America's Delta Force were deployed to Libya as analysts, instructing the rebels on specifics about weapons and tactics.[16] Ambassador J. Christopher Stevenswas named the first liaison with the Libyan opposition in March 2011. After the end of the war, both the CIA and the US State department were tasked with continuing to identify and collect arms that had flooded the country during the war, particularly shoulder-fired missiles taken from the former arsenal of the fallen regime of Gaddafi, as well as securing Libyan chemical weapon stockpiles, and helping to train Libya's new intelligence service.

Further, eastern Libya and Benghazi were key intelligence-gathering hubs for intelligence operatives. Before the attack, the CIA was monitoring Ansar al-Sharia and suspected members of Al-Qaeda in the Islamic Maghreb, as well as attempting to define the leadership and loyalty of the various militias present and their interaction with the Salafi elements of Libyan society. By the time of the attack, dozens of CIA operatives were on the ground in Benghazi. In addition, it has been reported that in the summer of 2012, AmericanJoint Special Operations Command (JSOC) missions had begun to target Libyan militias linked to the Al-Qaeda network of Yasin al-Suri.[58] By the time of the attack, a composite US Special Operations team with two JSOC members was already in Libya working on their mission profile independently of the CIA and State department operations.[58]

Multiple anonymous sources reported that the diplomatic mission in Benghazi was used by CIA as a cover to smuggle weapons from Libya to anti-Assad rebels in Syria.[56] Seymour Hersh cites a source among intelligence officials, saying *The consulate's only mission was to provide cover for the moving of arms. It had no real political role.* The attack allegedly brought end to active US involvement, but did not stop the smuggling. In January 2014, the House Permanent Select Committee on Intelligence reported that "All CIA activities in Benghazi were legal and authorized. On-the-record testimony establishes that CIA was not sending weapons ... from Libya to Syria, or facilitating other organizations or states that were transferring weapons from Libya to Syria."

During Congressional hearings, Ambassador Stevens' top deputy in Libya, Gregory N. Hicks, testified that Ambassador Stevens was in Benghazi in 2012 because "Secretary Clinton wanted the post made permanent," and it was understood that the secretary hoped to make an announcement to that effect during a visit to Tripoli later in the year. He also stated that "Chris wanted to make a symbolic gesture to the people of Benghazi that the United States stood behind their dream of establishing a new democracy."

Instability in Benghazi

- In April 2012, two former security guards for the consulate threw a homemade "fish bomb" IED over the consulate fence; the incident did not cause any casualties. Just 4 days later, a similar bomb was thrown at a four vehicle convoy carrying the United Nations Special Envoy to Libya, exploding just 12 feet from the UN envoy's vehicle without injuring anyone.

- In May 2012 an Al-Qaida affiliate calling itself the *Imprisoned Omar Abdul Rahman Brigades* claimed responsibility for an attack on the International Red Cross (ICRC) office in Benghazi. On August 6 the ICRC suspended operations in Benghazi. The head of the ICRC's delegation in Libya said the aid group was "appalled" by the attack and "extremely concerned" about escalating violence in Libya.

- The *Imprisoned Omar Abdul Rahman Brigades* released a video of what it said was its detonation of an explosive device outside the gates of the U.S. consulate on June 5, which caused no casualties but damaged the consulate's perimeter wall, described by one individual as "big enough for forty men to go through." The Brigades claimed that the attack was in response to the killing of Abu Yahya al Libi, a Libyan al-Qaeda leader who had just died in an American drone attack, and was also timed to coincide with the imminent arrival of a U.S. diplomat. There were no injuries, but the group left behind leaflets promising more attacks against the U.S.

- British ambassador to Libya Dominic Asquith survived an assassination attempt in Benghazi on June 10. Two British protection officers were injured in the attack when their convoy was hit by a rocket-propelled grenade 300 yards from their consulate office. The British Foreign Office withdrew all consular staff from Benghazi in late June.

- On June 18, 2012, the Tunisian consulate in Benghazi was stormed by individuals affiliated with Ansar Al-Sharia Libya, allegedly because of "attacks by Tunisian artists against Islam."[31]
- On the day of the attack: Two consulate security guards spotted a man in a Libyan police uniform taking pictures of the consulate with his cell phone from a nearby building that was under construction. The security guards briefly detained the man before releasing him. He drove away in a police car and a complaint was made to the Libyan police station.Sean Smith noticed this surveillance, posting on the internet "assuming we don't die tonight. We saw one of our 'police' that guard the compound taking pictures."[34]

According to a local security official, he and a battalion commander had met with U.S. diplomats three days before the attack and warned the Americans about deteriorating security in the area. The official told CNN that the diplomats had been advised, "The situation is frightening, it scares us."

Ambassador Stevens' diary, which was later found at the unsecured site of the attack, recorded his concern about the growing al-Qaeda presence in the area and his worry about being on an al-Qaeda hit list.

After a meeting to discuss the deteriorating security situation at the U.S. diplomatic compound in Benghazi, embassy officials in Tripoli drafted a cable on August 16 outlining the circumstances and specifying that security needs would be made known in a subsequent message. This cable, excerpts from which have been reported by Fox News, still remains classified. After reading it, Army General Carter Ham, then the head of the U.S. Africa Command and the senior U.S. military official in the region, phoned Stevens and asked if the compound needed a special security team from the U.S. military. Stevens told Ham it did not, according to two government officials. Weeks later, Stevens traveled to Germany for an already scheduled meeting with Ham at AFRICOM headquarters. During that meeting, Ham again offered additional military assets, and Stevens again said no, the two officials said. One anonymous source told a reporter from the McClatchy News Service that Stevens may have[dubious – discuss] declined the offers because there was an understanding in the State Department that consular officials should not request more security due to political concerns, since the country was being touted as a foreign policy success.

U.S. security officer, Eric Nordstrom, twice requested additional security for the mission in Benghazi from his superiors at the State Department. His requests were denied. According to Nordstrom, State Department official, Charlene Lamb, wanted to keep the security presence in Benghazi "artificially low". Secretary of State Hillary Clinton later took responsibility for the security lapses.

On December 30, 2012, the United States Senate Committee on Homeland Security and Governmental Affairs released a report, "Flashing Red: A Special Report on the Terrorist Attack at Benghazi," wherein it was determined:

In the months leading up to the attack on the Temporary Mission Facility in Benghazi, there was a large amount of evidence gathered by the U.S. Intelligence Community (IC) and from open sources that Benghazi was increasingly dangerous and unstable, and that a significant attack against American personnel there was becoming much more likely. While this intelligence was effectively shared within the Intelligence Community (IC) and with key officials at the Department of State, it did not lead to a commensurate increase in security at Benghazi nor to a decision to close the American mission there, either of which would have been more than justified by the intelligence presented....The RSO in Libya compiled a list of 234 security incidents in Libya between June 2011 and July 2012, 50 of which took place in Benghazi.

The Attack

The Benghazi attack consisted of military assaults on two separate U.S. diplomatic compounds. The first assault occurred at the main compound, approximately 300 yards long and 100 yards wide, at about 9:40 pm local time (3:40 pm EDT, Washington DC). The second assault took place at a CIA annex 1.2 miles away (coordinates 32.057186°N 20.087706°E) at about 4 am the following morning.

Assault on the Compound

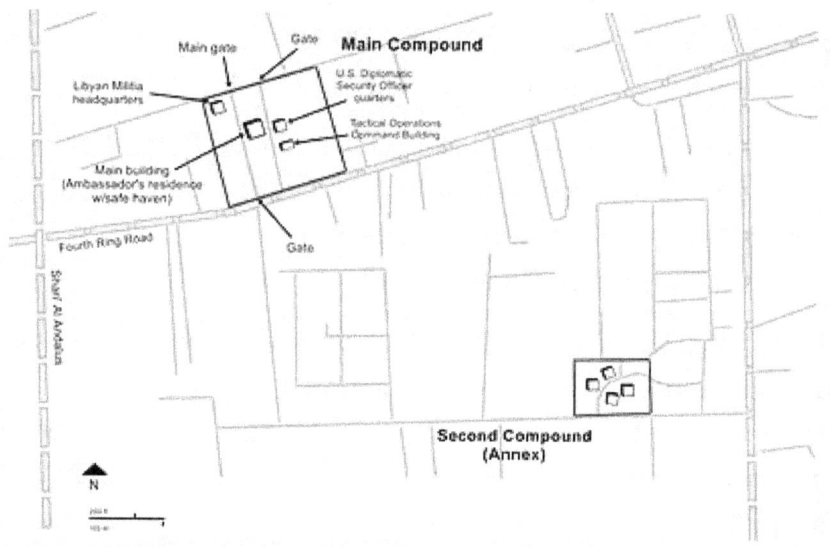

Map of the U.S. mission main compound and annex.

Between 125 and 150 gunmen, "some wearing the Afghan-style tunics favored by Islamic militants," are reported to have participated in the assault. Some had their faces covered and wore flak jackets.Weapons they used during the attack included rocket-propelled grenades (RPGs), hand grenades, AK-47 andFN F2000 NATO assault rifles, diesel canisters, mortars, and heavy machine guns and artillery mounted on gun trucks.

The assault began at nightfall, with the attackers sealing off streets leading to the main compound with gun trucks. The trucks bore the logo of Ansar al-Sharia, a group of Islamist militants working with the local government to manage security in Benghazi. (Ansar al-Sharia was listed in January 2014 by the U.S. Department of State as a terror organization.)

The area outside the compound before the assault was quiet; one Libyan guard who was wounded in the attack was quoted as saying "there wasn't a single ant outside." The attackers stated they were acting in response to the movie.[clarification needed] No more than seven Americans were in the compound, including Ambassador Stevens.

Stevens was visiting Benghazi at the time to review plans to establish a new cultural center and modernize a hospital. The ambassador also "needed to report ... on the physical and the political and security environment in Benghazi to support an action memo to convert Benghazi from a temporary facility to a permanent facility." Surplus funds originally dedicated for use in Iran for fiscal year 2012 were to be redirected and obligated for use in Benghazi: an action that had to be completed before the end of the fiscal year— September 30, 2012.

Ambassador Stevens had his last meeting of the day with a Turkish diplomat, and Stevens escorted the Turkish diplomat to the main gate at about 8:30 pm local time. The street outside the compound was calm, and the State Department reported no unusual activity during the day outside. Ambassador Stevens retired to his room at about 9 pm, where he reportedly remained alone in the building, according to guards interviewed later.

About 9:40 pm local time large numbers of armed men shouting "Allāhu Akbar" descended on the compound from multiple directions. The attackers lobbed grenades over the wall and entered the compound under a barrage of automatic weapons fire and RPGs, backed by truck-mounted artillery and anti-aircraft machine guns. A Diplomatic Security Service (DSS) agent viewed on the consulate's security cameras "a large number of men, armed men, flowing into the compound." He hit the alarm and started shouting, "Attack! Attack!" over the loudspeaker. Phone calls were made to the embassy in Tripoli, the Diplomatic Security Command Center in Washington, the Libyan February 17 Brigade, and a U.S. quick reaction force located at the annex compound a little more than a mile away. Ambassador Stevens telephoned Deputy Chief of Mission Gregory Hicks in Tripoli to tell him the consulate was under attack. Mr. Hicks did not recognize the phone number so he didn't answer it, twice. On the third attempt Mr. Hicks answered the call from Ambassador Stevens.

Diplomatic Security Service Special Agent Scott Strickland secured Ambassador Stevens and Sean Smith, an information management officer, in the main building's safe haven. Other agents retrieved their M4 carbines and tactical gear from another building. They tried to return to the main building but encountered armed attackers and retreated.

The attackers entered the main building and rattled the locked metal grille of the safe haven. They carried jerrycans of diesel fuel, spread the fuel over the floor and furniture, and set fires. As thick smoke filled the building, Stevens, Smith, and Strickland moved to the bathroom and lay on the floor, but they decided to leave the safe haven after being overcome by smoke. Strickland exited through the window, but Stevens and Smith did not follow him. Strickland returned several times but couldn't find them in the smoke; he went up to the roof and radioed other agents.

Three agents returned to the main building in an armored vehicle; they searched the building and found Smith's body, but not Stevens.

According Operators with the Annex Security Team, they had become aware of the consulate attack after 9:30 pm local time, and were ready to respond within five minutes, however they were delayed from responding by "the top CIA officer in Benghazi". The Regional Security Office sounded the alarm and placed calls to the Benghazi CIA annex and the embassy in Tripoli, saying, "We're under attack, we need help, please send help now ..." Then the call cut off. After some discussion, the CIA's Global Response Staff (GRS) at the CIA annex, which included senior security operative Tyrone S. Woods, decided to implement a rescue. By 10:05pm, the team was briefed and loaded into their armored Toyota Land Cruisers. By this time, communicators at the CIA annex were notifying the chain of command about current developments, and a small CIA and JSOC element in Tripoli that includedGlen Doherty was attempting to find a way to Benghazi.[39-43]

The GRS team from the CIA annex arrived at the consulate and attempted to secure the perimeter and locate the ambassador and Sean Smith. Diplomatic security agent David Ubben located Smith, who was unconscious and later declared dead, but the team was unable to find Stevens in the smoke-filled building. The team then decided to return to the annex with the survivors and Smith's body. While en route back to the annex, the group's armored vehicle was hit by AK-47 rifle fire and hand grenades. The vehicle was able to make it to its destination with two flat tires, and the gates to annex were closed behind them at 11:50pm.[43-45]

Abdel-Monem Al-Hurr, the spokesman for Libya's Supreme Security Committee, said roads leading to the Benghazi consulate compound were sealed off and Libyan state security forces had surrounded it.

A U.S. Army commando unit was sent to Naval Air Station Sigonella in Sicily, Italy the night of the attack but did not deploy to Benghazi. U.S. officials say the team did not arrive at Sigonella until after the attack was over.

Reaction in the United States

Diplomatic Security Service agents/Regional Security Officers informed their headquarters in Washington about the attack just as it was beginning at about 9:40 local time (3:40PM Eastern Time). By 4:30 Eastern, Pentagon officials informed Defense Secretary Leon Panetta about the attack. The Pentagon ordered an unmanned aerial vehicle that was in the air conducting surveillance on militant camps to fly over Benghazi. The drone arrived at 11:10 pm local time (5:10 pm Eastern Time) and began providing a video feed to Washington. At 5:41 pm Eastern Time, Secretary of State Hillary Clinton telephoned CIA Director David Petraeus to coordinate. The CIA, which made up most of the US government's presence in Benghazi, had a ten-member security team at its annex and the State Department believed that this team would assist the consulate in the event of an attack.

Recovery of Ambassador Stevens

Some of the Libyans who entered the compound apparently tried to rescue Stevens after they found him lying alone on the floor in a dark smoke-filled room with a locked door accessible only by a window. A group of men pulled him out of the room through the window, and then placed him on the courtyard's stone tile floor. The crowd cheered "God is great" when Stevens was found to be alive. A 22-year-old freelance videographer, Fahd al-Bakoush, later published a video showing Libyans trying to extract the unconscious ambassador from a smoke-filled room, where he was found unconscious. At around 1 am, he was then rushed to the Benghazi Medical Center, a hospital controlled by the Ansar Al-Sharia militia, in a private car as there was no ambulance to carry him.

At the hospital Stevens was administered CPR for 90 minutes by Dr. Ziad Abu Zeid. According to Abu Zeid, Stevens died from asphyxiation caused by smoke inhalation, and that Stevens had no other injuries. The doctor said he believed that officers from the

Libyan Interior Ministry transported the body to the airport and into United States custody. State Department officials said they do not know who took Stevens to the hospital or transported the body to the airport and into U.S. custody. Jack Murphy reported that in the absence of orders and on their own initiative, two JSOC operators from the composite U.S. Special Operations team that was already in Libya before the attack left their safe house to search for Ambassador Stevens after they heard about the attack. They drove into Benghazi, located Stevens's remains at the hospital controlled by Ansar Al-Sharia, and recovered it after an exchange of gunfire.

Assault on the CIA annex

Just after midnight, an attack on the CIA annex began, which included machine gun, rocket and mortar fire. The CIA defenses held off the attack until the morning of September 12.[45–46] Early in the morning, Libyan government forces met up with a group of Americans, reinforcements from Tripoli including Glen Doherty, that had arrived at the Benghazi airport. The team, which included two active-duty JSOC operators and five CIA personnel, had commandeered a small jet in Tripoli by paying the pilots $30,000 and forcing them to fly the team to Benghazi.[43] After being held up at the airport for a few hours, the Libyan forces and newly arrived Americans went to the CIA annex at about 5:00am to assist in transporting approximately 32 Americans at the annex back to the airport for evacuation. Minutes after they drove through the gates, the annex came under heavy fire. The team immediately took up defensive positions. With a lull in the fighting, Glen Doherty began searching for his friend, Tyrone S. Woods, and he was told he was on the roof manning a MK46 machine gun. He found Woods on the roof with two other agents, they quickly embraced, filled each other in, and retook defensive firing positions. After only a few minutes, a mortar round hit Woods' position, fatally wounding him. As Doherty attempted to reposition and take cover, a second round fell on him, killing him instantly.[46–47] 31-year-oldDiplomatic Security Service Special Agent David Ubben suffered shrapnel injuries and several broken bones in the mortar attacks, and according to Ubben's father, "The first dropped 50 yards short and the next two were right on target."

Immediately, several agents ran onto the roof to assess damage and help the wounded, who were taken from the roof with a ladder. At the same time, a JSOC operator was using a hand-held device displaying images from a Predator drone above, which had been sent by the DOD's Africa Command after request. The operator told the Chief of Base, "There's a large element assembling, and we need to get everyone out of here now!" Evacuation was agreed upon, and everyone was notified to collect their personal security items and evacuate. Within minutes, vehicles were loaded, and they headed to the airport. On the way, they were hit with small arms fire, but arrived with no further injuries.[47–48]

During the fighting, the CIA had successfully rescued six State Department personnel, recovered Smith's body, and had evacuated about thirty Americans out of Benghazi alive. "Benghazi: The Definitive Report" claims that just under 100 attackers were killed.[46, 48]

Evacuation

The bodies were taken to Benina International Airport and flown to the capital, Tripoli, and then to Ramstein Air Base in Germany aboard a C-17 military transport aircraft. From Germany, the four bodies arrived at Andrews Air Force Base near Washington, D.C., where President Barack Obama and members of his cabinet held a ceremony in honor of those killed.

After the attack, all diplomatic staff were moved to the capital, Tripoli, with nonessential personnel to be flown out of Libya. Sensitive documents remained missing, including documents listing the names of Libyans working with the Americans, and documents relating to oil contracts.

Fatalities and injuries

Four Americans died in the attack: Ambassador Stevens, Information Officer Sean Smith, and two CIA operatives, Glen Doherty and Tyrone Woods, both former Navy SEALs. Stevens is the first U.S. ambassador killed in an attack since Adolph Dubs was killed in 1979. Senior intelligence officials later acknowledged that Woods and Doherty were contracted by the Central Intelligence Agency, not the State Department as previously identified, and were part of a Global Response Staff (GRS), a team that provides security to CIA case officers and countersurveillance and surveillance protection.

Initial reports indicated that ten Libyan guards died; this was later retracted and it was reported that seven Libyans were injured. An early report indicated that three Americans were injured in the attack and treated at an American Military Hospital in Germany.

Since then, reports differ regarding the number of Americans wounded in the attacks. The ARB report released December 20, 2012 stated that 2 Americans were wounded. In March 2013 it was reported that the State Department said there were 4 injured Americans. And in August 2013, CNN reported that 7 Americans were wounded, some seriously.

Glen Doherty

Glen Anthony Doherty (c. 1970 – September 11, 2012) of Encinitas, was a native of Winchester, Massachusetts, and a 1988 graduate of Winchester High School. Doherty was the second of three children born to Bernard and Barbara Doherty. He trained as a pilot at Embry–Riddle Aeronautical University before moving to Snowbird, Utah for several winters and then joining the United States Navy. Doherty served as a Navy SEAL, responded to the bombing of the USS *Cole*, had tours of duty in Iraq and Afghanistan, and left the Navy in 2005 as a petty officer, first class. After leaving the Navy, he worked for a private security company in Afghanistan, Iraq, Israel, Kenya and Libya. In the month prior to the attack, Doherty as a contractor with the State Department told ABC News in an interview that he personally went into the field in Libya to track down MANPADS, shoulder-fired surface-to-air missiles, and destroy them.

Doherty was a member of the advisory board of the Military Religious Freedom Foundation, an organization that opposes proselytizing by religious groups in the United States military. Doherty was co-author of the book *The 21st Century Sniper*.

Doherty's funeral was held at Saint Eulalia's parish in his native Winchester on September 19, 2012. His celebration of life was held in Encinitas, California the weekend of October 12–14, 2012.

Tyrone S. Woods

Tyrone Snowden Woods (January 15, 1971 – September 12, 2012), of Imperial Beach, was born in Portland, Oregon. Woods graduated from Oregon City High School in 1989, south of Portland, Oregon, and served 20 years of honorable service in the U.S. Navy before joining State Department Diplomatic Security as a U.S. embassy security personnel, ostensibly working under a service contract. Since 2010, Woods had protected American diplomats in posts from Central America to the Middle East. In November 2012, senior U.S. intelligence officials said that Woods and Doherty were actually CIA contractors, not State Department security officers as had been previously reported, and that the two men, together with other CIA security officers, played a pivotal role in defending against the Benghazi embassy attack.

As a Navy SEAL in 2005–06, Woods was awarded the Bronze Star Medal with combat "V" Device for valor in Iraq. He led 12 direct action raids and 10 reconnaissance missions leading to the capture of 34 enemy insurgents in the volatile Al Anbar province. He served multiple tours in Iraq and Afghanistan, the Middle East and Central America. He retired as a senior chief petty officer in 2010.

Woods also served with distinction at the Naval Medical Center San Diego as a registered nurse and certified paramedic. Having settled in Imperial Beach, California, for a year of his retirement he owned The Salty Frog bar there; he is survived by his second wife, Dr. Dorothy Narvaez-Woods, their one child, and two sons from a previous marriage. Woods was buried at Fort Rosecrans National Cemetery.

Responsibility

On September 10, 2012, at least 18 hours before the attack in Benghazi, al-Qaeda leader Ayman al-Zawahiri released a video to coincide with the anniversary of the 9/11 attacks in 2001, which called for attacks on Americans in Libya in order to avenge the death of Abu Yahya al-Libi in a drone strike in Pakistan in June 2012. It is uncertain how much prior knowledge of the attack al-Zawahiri had, though he praised the attackers on October 12, 2012 in another video. On September 14, 2012, al-Qaeda in the Arabian Peninsulareleased a statement arguing the attack was revenge for the death of al-Libi, though they did not claim official responsibility for the Benghazi attack. It was later reported that 3 operatives from the group did take part in the attack. Further, an intercepted phone call from the Benghazi area immediately after the attack reportedly linked senior Al-Qaeda in the Islamic Maghreb commander Mokhtar Belmokhtar to the attack.

David Kirkpatrick of the *New York Times* reported that 20-year-old neighbor Mohamed Bishari witnessed the attack. According to Bishari, it was launched without warning or protest and was led by the Islamist militia Ansar al-Sharia (different from the group called Ansar al-Sharia based in Yemen designated by the U.N. and the U.S. Department of State as a terrorist organization). Kirkpatrick reported that Ansar al-Sharia said they were launching the assault in retaliation for the release of the anti-Islamic video, *Innocence of Muslims*. It was further reported that Ahmed Abu Khattala was called a ringleader of the attack by both witnesses and authorities, though he insisted he did not play a part in the aggression at the American compound. Witnesses, Benghazi residents, and Western news reports have described him as a leader of Ansar al-Sharia, though he stated he was close to the group but not an official part of it. He further stated he was the commander of an Islamist brigade, Abu Obaida ibn al-Jarrah, some of whose members had joined Ansar al-Sharia.

The imprisoned Omar Abdul Rahman Brigades, a pro-al-Qaeda militia calling for the release of The Blind Sheik, was implicated in the attack by Noman Benotman of the Quilliam Foundation. CNN, the Carnegie Endowment for International Peace, Commentary Magazine and The Daily Telegraph have listed this group as a chief suspect. USA Today reported that protests in Cairo which preceded the attack on Benghazi were intended to protest the imprisonment of Sheik Omar Abdul Rahman and announced as early as August 30. Egyptian President Mohammed Morsi had called for release of the Blind Sheikh in his inaugural address.

In the days and weeks following the attack, President Obama and other administration officials noted that the video had sparked violent incidents at a number of U.S. diplomatic facilities and stated it was also a prime catalyst for the Benghazi attack. Two days after the attack, CNN reporter Sarah Aarthun quoted an anonymous senior U.S. administration official: "It was not an innocent mob. The video or 9/11 made a handy excuse and could be fortuitous from their perspective but this was a clearly planned military-type attack." In his September 18 appearance on The Late Show with David Letterman, President Obama said that "extremists and terrorists used (the anti-Muslim YouTube video) as an excuse to attack a variety of our embassies." In his Univision Town Hall appearance on September 20, President Obama said that the "natural protests that arose because of the outrage over the video were used as an excuse by extremists to see if they can also directly harm U.S. interests." A later report from an independent review board concluded "there was no protest prior to the attacks."

In October 2012, a Tunisian Ali Harzi, who a US intelligence official stated had links to Ansar al-Sharia and al-Qaeda in the Maghreb, was arrested in Turkey and repatriated to Tunisia on terrorism charges and possible links to the attack on the US embassy in Benghazi. Ali Harzi was released by Tunisian authorities on January 8, 2013 due to lack of evidence.

Also in October, a Libyan suspect, Karim el-Azizi, who had recently returned to Egypt from Libya and was storing weapons in his hideout, detonated a bomb and was found dead in his apartment after clashes with security forces. He has been linked to an Egyptian terrorist group led by Muhammad Jamal Abu Ahmad, who is suspected of training some of the terrorists responsible for the Benghazi attack in camps in the Libyan desert. Jamal Abu Ahmad, a former member of Egyptian Islamic Jihad, was released from Egyptian prison after the fall of the Mubarak regime, after which he began assembling a terrorist network. He received financing from the Yemen-based Al-Qaeda in the Arabian Peninsula, petitioned Al-Qaeda leader Ayman al-Zawahiri to establish a new Al-Qaeda affiliate he called al-Qaeda in Egypt, and was subsequently detained by Egyptian authorities in December 2012. On October 7, 2013, the Muhammad Jamal network (MJN) and Muhammad Jamal were designated as "global terrorists" by the U.S. Department of State. The U.S. State Department noted in its designation that Jamal "has developed connections with al-Qa'ida in the Islamic Maghreb (AQIM), AQ senior leadership, and al-Qa'ida in the Arabian Peninsula (AQAP) leadership including Nasir 'Abd-al-Karim 'Abdullah al-Wahishi and Qasim Yahya Mahdi al-Rimi." A few days later, on October 21, 2013, the United Nations Security Council designated the MJN "as being associated with Al-Qaida." The United Nations Security Council also noted, "Some of the attackers of the U.S. Mission in Benghazi on September 11, 2012 have been identified as associates of Muhammad Jamal, and some of the Benghazi attackers reportedly trained at MJN camps in Libya."

In March 2013, Faraj al-Shibli was detained by Libyan authorities and questioned by the FBI due to his suspected involvement in the Benghazi attack. Al-Shibli was detained after he returned from a trip to Pakistan, though his exact role in the attack is unclear. He was a member of the Libyan Islamic Fighting Group, which tried to overthrow the Gadhafi regime in the mid-1990s. Investigators have learned he has had contact with both the Yemen-based Al-Qaeda in the Arabian Peninsula and Al-Qaeda members in Pakistan. He was released by Libyan authorities on June 12, 2013 based on claims there was a lack of evidence to hold him in custody. In July 2014 he was found dead in Libya.

Aftermath

Libyan response

Libyan Prime Minister Mustafa Abushagur's office condemned the attack and extended condolences, saying: "While strongly condemning any attempt to abuse the person of Muhammad, or an insult to our holy places and prejudice against the faith, we reject and strongly condemn the use of force to terrorize innocent people and the killing of innocent people." It also reaffirmed "the depth of relationship between the peoples of Libya and the U.S., which grew closer with the positions taken by the U.S. government in support of the revolution of February 17." Mohamed Yousef el-Magariaf, the President of the General National Congress of Libya, said: "We apologise to the United States, the people and to the whole world for what happened. We confirm that no-one will escape from punishment and questioning."

There were demonstrations in Benghazi and Tripoli on September 12, condemning the violence and holding signs such as "Chris Stevens was a friend to all Libyans," "Benghazi is against terrorism," and other signs apologizing to Americans for the actions in their name and in the name of Muslims. On the same day, Libya's Deputy Ambassador to London Ahmad Jibril told the BBC that Ansar Al-Sharia was behind the attack. On September 13, at a US State Department reception in Washington D.C., the Libyan ambassador to the US Ali Aujali apologized to Secretary of State Clinton for "this terrorist attack which took place against the American consulate in Libya." The ambassador further praised Stevens as a "dear friend" and a "real hero". He also urged the United States to continue supporting Libya as it went "through a very difficult time" and that the young Libyan government needed help so that it could "maintain ... security and stability in our country."

In the days after the attack, *The New York Times* stated that young Libyans had flooded Twitter with pro-American messages after the attacks. *Think Progress* stated that Libyans are typically more positively inclined towards the United States than their neighbors. A 2012 Gallup poll noted that "A majority of Libyans (54%) surveyed in March and April 2012 approve of the leadership of the U.S. – among the highest approval Gallup has ever recorded in the ... region, outside of Israel." Another poll in Eastern Libya, taken in 2011, reported that the population was at the same time both deeply religious conservative Muslims and very pro-American, with 90% of respondents reporting favorable views of the United States.

The Libyan response to the crisis was praised and appreciated in the United States, and President Obama emphasized how the Libyans "helped our diplomats to safety" to an American audience the following day, while a *New York Times* editorial criticized Egypt's government for not doing "what Libyan leaders did."

On September 16, Libyan President Mohamed Magariaf said that the attack on the U.S. consulate was planned months in advance, and further stated that "he idea that this criminal and cowardly act was a spontaneous protest that just spun out of control is completely unfounded and preposterous. We firmly believe that this was a precalculated, preplanned attack that was carried out specifically to attack the U.S. consulate."

Anti-militia demonstrations

On September 21, about 30,000 Libyans marched through Benghazi calling for support of the rule of law and for an end to the armed militias that had formed during the Libyan civil war to oppose Colonel Gaddafi. After that war, the militias failed to disband, and continually menaced the Libyan government and populace. Carrying signs with slogans such as "We Want Justice For Chris" and "Libya Lost a Friend," the protestors stormed several militia headquarters, including that of Ansar al-Sharia, an Islamist militia who some allege played a role in the attack on U.S. diplomatic personnel on September 11. At least 10 people were killed and dozens more wounded as militiamen fired on demonstrators at the headquarters of Sahaty Brigade, a pro-government militia "operating under the authority of the ministry of defence."

By early next morning, the protestors had forced militia members to flee and seized control of a number of compounds, releasing four prisoners found inside. Protesters burnt a car and a building of at least one facility, and looted weapons. The militia compounds and many weapons were handed over to Libya's national army in what "appeared to be part of a coordinated sweep of militia bases by police, government troops and activists" following the earlier demonstrations. Some militia members accused the protestors of being Gaddafi loyalists, looking to disarm the militias in the wake of the revolution.

Government campaign to disband militias

On September 23, taking advantage of the growing momentum and rising anger against the militias evinced in the earlier anti-militia demonstrations, the Libyan president declared that all unauthorized militias had 48 hours to either disband or come under government control. The government also mandated that bearing arms in public was now illegal, as were armed checkpoints.

It has been noted that previously, handling the militias had been difficult as the government had been forced to rely on some of them for protection and security. According to a Libyan interviewed in Tripoli, the government gained the ability to push back against the militias because of a "mandate of the people."

On the 24th, the government commenced with a raid on a former military base held by a rogue infantry militia.

Across the country, militias began surrendering to the government. The government formed a "National Mobile Force" for the purpose of evicting illegal militias. On the same day as the declaration, various militias in Misrata held meetings, ultimately deciding to submit to the government's authority, and handed over various public facilities they had been holding, including the city's three main jails, which were handed over to the authority of the Ministry of Justice. Hours before the announcement, in Derna, the two main militias (one of them Ansar al-Sharia) active in the city both withdrew, leaving both their five military bases behind.

Hundreds of Libyans, mainly former rebel fighters, gathered in the city centers of Tripoli and Benghazi to hand over their weapons to the government on the 29th of September.

The campaign has been less successful in other areas, such as the remote Nafusa Mountains, inhabited by the Nafusi-speaking Berber minority, where the Emirati news agency The National reported on 23 September that arms were being hoarded. The National also reported arms being hoarded in Misrata, despite simultaneous reporting by other outlets that militias were surrendering in Misrata.

U.S. government response

On September 12, U.S. President Barack Obama condemned "this outrageous attack" on U.S. diplomatic facilities and stated that "ince our founding, the United States has been a nation that respects all faiths. We reject all efforts to denigrate the religious beliefs of others." After referring to "the 9/11 attacks," "troops who made the ultimate sacrifice in Iraq and Afghanistan", and "then last night, we learned the news of this attack in Benghazi" the President urged, "As Americans, let us never, ever forget that our freedom is only sustained because there are people who are willing to fight for it, to stand up for it, and in some cases, lay down their lives for it." He then went on to say, "No acts of terror will ever shake the resolve of this great nation, alter that character, or eclipse the light of the values that we stand for. Today we mourn four more Americans who represent the very best of the United States of America. We will not waver in our commitment to see that justice is done for this terrible act. And make no mistake, justice will be done."

After the attack, Obama ordered that security be increased at all such facilities worldwide. A 50-member Marine FAST team was sent to Libya to "bolster security." It was announced that the FBI would investigate the possibility of the attack being planned. U.S. officials said surveillance over Libya would increase, including the use of unmanned drones, to "hunt for the attackers."

Secretary of State Clinton also made a statement on September 12, describing the perpetrators as "heavily armed militants" and "a small and savage group – not the people or government of Libya." She also reaffirmed "America's commitment to religious tolerance" and said "Some have sought to justify this vicious behavior, along with the protest that took place at our Embassy in Cairo yesterday, as a response to inflammatory material posted on the internet," but whether true or not, that was not a justification for violence. The State Department had previously identified embassy and personnel security as a major challenge in its budget and priorities report.

On September 12, it was reported that the United States Navy dispatched two *Arleigh Burke* class destroyers, the USS *McFaul* and the USS *Laboon*, to the Libyan coast. The destroyers are equipped with Tomahawk cruise missiles. American UAVs were also sent to fly over Libya to search for the perpetrators of the attack.

In a speech on September 13, in Golden, Colorado, President Obama paid tribute to the four Americans "killed in an attack on our diplomatic post in Libya," stating, "We enjoy our security and our liberty because of the sacrifices they make ... I want people around the world to hear me: To all those who would do us harm, no act of terror will go unpunished. It will not dim the light of the values that we proudly present to the rest of the world."

In his press briefing on September 14, White House Press Secretary Jay Carney told reporters that "we don't have and did not have concrete evidence to suggest that this was not in reaction to the film." He went on to say: "There was no intelligence that in any way could have been acted on to prevent these attacks. It is – I mean, I think the DNI spokesman was very declarative about this that the report is false. The report suggested that there was intelligence that was available prior to this that led us to believe that this facility would be attacked, and that is false ... We have no information to suggest that it was a preplanned attack. The unrest we've seen around the region has been in reaction to a video that Muslims, many Muslims find offensive. And while the violence is reprehensible and unjustified, it is not a reaction to the 9/11 anniversary that we know of, or to U.S. policy."

On September 14 the remains of the slain Americans were returned to the U.S. President Obama and Secretary of State Hillary Clinton attended the ceremony. In her remarks Clinton said, "One young woman, her head covered and her eyes haunted with sadness, held up a handwritten sign that said 'Thugs and killers don't represent Benghazi nor Islam.' The President of the Palestinian Authority, who worked closely with Chris when he served in Jerusalem, sent me a letter remembering his energy and integrity, and deploring – and I quote – 'an act of ugly terror.'" She went on to say: "We've seen the heavy assault on our post in Benghazi that took the lives of those brave men."

On September 16, the U.S. Ambassador to the U.N. Susan Rice appeared on five major interview shows to discuss the attacks. Prior to her appearance, Rice was provided with "talking points" from a CIA memo, which stated:

The currently available information suggests that the demonstrations in Benghazi were spontaneously inspired by the protests at the U.S. Embassy in Cairo and evolved into a direct assault against the U.S. diplomatic post in Benghazi and subsequently its annex. There are indications that extremists participated in the violent demonstrations.

This assessment may change as additional information is collected and analyzed and as currently available information continues to be evaluated. The investigation is ongoing, and the U.S. government is working with Libyan authorities to bring to justice those responsible for the deaths of U.S. citizens.

Using these talking points as a guide, Rice stated:

Based on the best information we have to date, what our assessment is as of the present is in fact what began spontaneously in Benghazi as a reaction to what had transpired some hours earlier in Cairo where, of course, as you know, there was a violent protest outside of our embassy—sparked by this hateful video. But soon after that spontaneous protest began outside of our consulate in Benghazi, we believe that it looks like extremist elements, individuals, joined in that-- in that effort with heavy weapons of the sort that are, unfortunately, readily now available in Libya post-revolution. And that it spun from there into something much, much more violent." "We do not-- we do not have information at present that leads us to conclude that this was premeditated or preplanned." "I think it's clear that there were extremist elements that joined in and escalated the violence. Whether they were al Qaeda affiliates, whether they were Libyan-based extremists or al Qaeda itself I think is one of the things we'll have to determine.

In a White House press briefing on September 18, press secretary Jay Carney explained the attack to reporters: "I'm saying that based on information that we – our initial information, and that includes all information – we saw no evidence to back up claims by others that this was a preplanned or premeditated attack; that we saw evidence that it was sparked by the reaction to this video. And that is what we know thus far based on the evidence, concrete evidence."

On September 20, White House Press Secretary Jay Carney answered a question about an open hearing with the National Counterterrorism Center Director, Matthew G. Olsen, which referenced which extremist groups might have been involved. Carney said, "It is, I think, self-evident that what happened in Benghazi was a terrorist attack. Our embassy was attacked violently, and the result was four deaths of American officials. So, again, that's self-evident." On the same day, during an appearance on Univision, a Spanish-language television network in the United States, President Obama stated, "What we do know is that the natural protests that arose because of the outrage over the video were used as an excuse by extremists to see if they can also directly harm U.S. interests."

On September 24, advertisements condemning an anti-Islam video appeared on Pakistani television. The television ads in Pakistan (marked with the U.S. Embassy seal) feature clips of President Obama and Secretary of State Clinton during press appearances in Washington in which they condemned the video. Their words were subtitled in Urdu.

On September 25, in an address before the United Nations General Assembly President Obama stated, "The attacks on our civilians in Benghazi were attacks on America ... And there should be no doubt that we will be relentless in tracking down the killers and bringing them to justice." He referred to *Innocence of Muslims* as "a crude and disgusting video sparked outrage throughout the Muslim world." He said, "I have made it clear that the United States government had nothing to do with this video, and I believe its message must be rejected by all who respect our common humanity." He further stated, "There is no video that justifies an attack on an Embassy."

On September 26, Clinton acknowledged a possible link between Al-Qaeda in the Islamic Maghreb and the Benghazi attack.

On September 28, it was reported that Nakoula Basseley Nakoula, the producer of the *Innocence of Muslims* video, had been arrested in California and was being held without bail.

On September 28, a spokesman for the Director of National Intelligence stated "In the immediate aftermath, there was information that led us to assess that the attack began spontaneously following protests earlier that day at our embassy in Cairo. We provided that initial assessment to Executive Branch officials and members of Congress ... As we learned more about the attack, we revised our initial assessment to reflect new information indicating that it was a deliberate and organized terrorist attack carried out by extremists. It remains unclear if any group or person exercised overall command and control of the attack, and if extremist group leaders directed their members to participate."

On October 4, 22 days after the attack, FBI investigators were finally allowed access to the scene of the attack. The crime scene was not secured during that time; neither American nor Libyan investigators were able to secure the scene. The hearing testimony revealed that "Hicks argued that Rice's comments so insulted the Libyan president -- since they contradicted his Sept. 16 claims that the attack was premeditated -- that it slowed the FBI's investigation. 'President Magariaf was insulted in front of his own people, in front of the world.

His credibility was reduced,' Hicks said, adding that the president was apparently 'still steamed' two weeks later."

Clinton was scheduled to testify before Congress on December 20 about the attack. On December 15, it was reported that she had become dehydrated from the flu, fainted, and sustained a concussion. Consequently her testimony was postponed. The incident prompted Republican rep. Allen West to claim that the illness was a ruse intended to avoid testifying. Former UN Ambassador John Bolton called the concussion a "diplomatic illness". After Clinton was later admitted to the hospital with a blood clot, these claims were criticized as a conspiracy theory.

On January 23, 2013, during testimony at a Senate hearing on Benghazi, Clinton engaged in a heated exchange with Senator Ron Johnson. When Johnson pressed her to explain why, in the immediate aftermath, no one from the State Department had asked American evacuees if there had been a protest before the attack, Clinton replied: "With all due respect, the fact is, we had four dead Americans! Was it because of a protest or was it because of guys out for a walk one night and decided they'd go kill some Americans?! What difference, at this point, does it make?! It is our job to figure out what happened and do everything we can to prevent it from ever happening again, Senator. Now, honestly, I will do my best to answer your questions about this, but the fact is that people were trying in real time to get to the best information. The has a process, I understand, going with the other committees to explain how these talking points came out. But you know, to be clear, it is, from my perspective, less important today looking backwards as to why these militants decided they did it than to find them and bring them to justice, and then maybe we'll figure out what was going on in the meantime." To assist the Libyan government in disbanding extremist groups, the Obama administration allocated $8 million to begin building an elite Libyan commando force over the next year.

In March, 2013, Representative Duncan D. Hunter introduced legislation into the 113th Congress to authorize awarding of Congressional Gold Medals to Doherty and Woods for their actions which led to their deaths. On July 30, 2013 Rep. Edward R. Royce (R, CA-39) introduced the Department of State Operations and Embassy Security Authorization Act, Fiscal Year 2014 (H.R. 2848; 113th Congress). Supporters argued that "this bill advances efforts to improve the physical infrastructure at posts overseas to comply with the highest standards of protection; to increase training for those responsible for guarding our compounds and personnel; to put in place procedures that respond appropriately to threats, reducing the chances of another attack like that suffered in Benghazi, Libya; to review the policies and procedures of the Bureau of Diplomatic Security; to authorize the use of *best value* contracting at high risk, high threat posts; to authorize security improvements at soft targets; and to provide for security enhancements in line with Accountability Review Board recommendations."

Critics including Republican Party members accused the Obama White House and State Department of over-emphasizing or fabricating the role of Islamic anger over the anti-Islamic movie *Innocence of Muslims* and alleged that the administration was reluctant to label the attack as "terrorist". Representative Mike Rogers (R-MI), chairman of the House Intelligence Committee, who on the 13th of September said that the attacks had all the hallmarks of a coordinated attack by al-Qaeda, has questioned whether there were any protests at all in Benghazi, saying: "I have seen no information that shows that there was a protest going on as you have seen around any other embassy at the time. It was clearly designed to be an attack." According to critics, the consulate site should have been secured better both before and after the attack.

On September 20, Secretary of State Hillary Clinton gave a classified briefing to U.S. Senators, which several Republican attendees criticized. According to the article, senators were angered at the

Obama administration's rebuff of their attempts to learn details of the Benghazi attack, only to see that information published the next day in *The New York Times* and *The Wall Street Journal.*

GOP legislators also took issue with delays in the investigation, which CNN attributed to "bureaucratic infighting" between the FBI, Justice, and State. On 26 September, SenatorJohnny Isakson (R-Georgia) said he "cannot believe that the FBI is not on the ground yet."

On CNN's *State of the Union with Candy Crowley* on September 30, Crowley observed that "Friday we got the administration's sort of definitive statement that this now looks as though it was a pre-planned attack by a terrorist group, some of whom were at least sympathetic to al Qaeda," and asked the senior Republican on the Senate Armed Services Committee, Senator John McCain, "why do you think and are you bothered that it has taken them this long from September 11th to now to get to this conclusion?" to which McCain replied that "it interferes with the depiction that the administration is trying to convey that al Qaeda is on the wane ... how else could you trot out our U.N. ambassador to say this was a spontaneous demonstration? ... It was either willful ignorance or abysmal intelligence to think that people come to spontaneous demonstrations with heavy weapons, mortars, and the attack goes on for hours."

In the Presidential debate of October 16, 2012, between President Obama and Mitt Romney, Romney claimed that "it took the president 14 days before he called the attack in Benghazi an act of terror." President Obama responded, "The day after the attack, governor, I stood in the Rose Garden and I told the American people and the world that we are going to find out exactly what happened," Obama said. "That this was an act of terror, and I also said that we're going to hunt down those who committed this crime." When Romney challenged Obama, asking "You said in the Rose Garden the day after the attack, it was an act of terror. It was not a spontaneous demonstration, is that what you're saying?", the President responded, "Please proceed, governor" and "Get the transcript." The moderator of the debate, Candy Crowley, agreed, stating "He -- he did call it an act of terror." In response to criticism from conservative media sources, CNN published a fact check article that supported the accuracy of Crowley's statements with portions of transcripts from the debate and Obama's Rose Garden speech.

On May 13, 2013, President Obama stated during a news conference, "The day after it happened, I acknowledged that this was an act of terrorism." This claim was disputed by Glenn Kessler of the *Washington Post* in a "Fact Checker" article, which explored at length the difference in meaning between the phrases "act of terror" and "act of terrorism." In the article, Kessler accused Obama of "revisionist history" for stating he had called the attack an "act of terrorism" when it fact he had used the term "act of terror."

On CBS's *Face the Nation* on October 28, Senator John McCain (R-AZ) stated that "this is either a massive cover-up or incompetence" and suggested that it was a scandal worse than Watergate. McCain stated, "we know that there were tapes, recordings inside the consulate during this fight ... So the president went on various shows, despite what he said in the Rose Garden, about terrorist acts, he went on several programs, including *The View,* including *Letterman,* including before the UN where he continued to refer, days later, many days later, to this as a spontaneous demonstration because of a hateful video. We know that is patently false. What did the president know? When did he know it? And what did he do about it?" CBS News reported earlier on October 24 that the video of the assault was recovered 20 days after the attack, from the more than 10 security cameras at the compound. In a radio interview October 29, 2012, Senator John McCain said that the surveillance tapes had been classified top secret.

Testimony from top U.S. commanders after the attack revealed that the military was unprepared for conflict across Africa and the Middle

East. No attack aircraft had been placed on high alert on September 11, the anniversary of the 9/11 attacks, and the closest fighter planes to trouble spots in North Africa were based in Aviano, Italy. The fighter planes based in Aviano were unarmed and no aerial refueling planes were within a 10 hour flight to the base. In addition, no AC-130 gunships were within a 10 hour flight of Libya, and their crews did not reach a staging base in Italy until 19 hours after the attack began.

In April 2013, the Pentagon announced the activation of a USMC quick response force for North Africa which would use the range and speed of the Bell Boeing V-22 Osprey to be able to respond to similar events in the future. Spain authorized the basing of the quick response force at Morón Air Base near Seville, for a temporary one-year term.

With the attack and subsequent criticism occurring in the last two months of the 2012 United States Presidential election, Democrats and liberal media figures accused Republicans of politicizing the attacks in an unprecedented manner. Romney was accused by the Obama campaign of trying to exploit the attacks for political gain, leading the father of Ambassador Stevens to call for both campaigns to avoid making it a campaign issue.

On October 19, 2012, House Oversight Committee Chairman Darrell Issa (R-CA) came under fire from intelligence officials in the Obama administration when he posted, on a public website, 166 pages of sensitive but unclassified State Department communications related to Libya. According to officials, the release of the unredacted documents compromised the identities of several Libyans working with the U.S. government and placed their lives in danger.

Robert Gates, former CIA director and Defense Secretary under Republican Presidents and then President Obama until stepping down in July 2011, has said that some critics of the government's response have a "cartoonish" view of military capabilities. He stated that he would have responded with equal caution given the risks and the lack of intelligence on the ground, and that American forces require planning and preparation which the circumstances did not allow for.

President Obama called the criticism a "sideshow" and later accused Congress of "taking its eye off the ball" on the subject of the economy and focusing on "phony scandals." White House Spokesman Jay Carney later specified that the criticism of the administration's handling of the Benghazi attacks was one of those "phony scandals".

U.S. media response

The Center for Media and Public Affairs at George Mason University described the conclusions of an unpublished study on November 2, 2012. Based on a textual analysis which tallied the occurrence of certain words and phrases in news reports, the study concluded that leading newspapers in the U.S. framed the attack in terms of a spontaneous protest as framed by the Obama administration's version, four times as often as a planned terrorist attack which was the Republican version.

Soon after the attack, Steve Kroft of CBS' 60 Minutes asked President Obama what he thought of the situation. The President avoided the question and would not to call the event terrorism. The exchange was not released until days before the 2012 presidential elections. Journalist Bret Baier, host of *Special Report with Bret Baier*, noted "Obama would not say whether he thought the attack was terrorism. Yet he would later emphasize at a presidential debate that in the Rose Garden the same day, he had declared the attack an act of terror." Baier also states: "Two days before the election, CBS posted additional portions of a Sept. 12 "60 Minutes" interview where President Obama seems to contradict himself on the Benghazi attack". as well as "Remember this is from a president who has been saying he was calling Benghazi a terrorist attack from the very first moment in the Rose Garden. Also, remember what he said in the debate and notice the new part. KROFT: Mr. President, this morning you went out of your way to avoid the use of the word terrorism in connection with the Libya Attack, do you believe that this was a terrorism attack? OBAMA: Well it's too early to tell exactly how this came about, what group was involved, but obviously it was an attack on Americans. And we are going to be working with the Libyan government to make sure that we bring these folks to justice, one way or the other".

Analyst Brit Hume said to CBS News that media bias is real in regards to Benghazi and if a Republican were president, there would have been much more critical and aggressive reporting. On September 13, Rachel Maddow, during her show on MSNBC, stated: "An organized attack. Anybody who tells you that what happened to our ambassador and our consulate in Libya was as a result of a protest over an offensive movie, you should ask them why they think that. That`s the first version of events we heard. That does not seem to explain what happened that night or by the facts or the more facts we get". On June 2014, Maddow criticized the right-wing media for reporting an arrest as bad news, said that Americas are poorly served by the media, and that "the take on Fox News is that's not actually news" and now "they have to make it bad news, they have to make into maybe a scandal itself."

On the October 24 edition of Fox News' *Special Report with Bret Baier*, syndicated columnist Charles Krauthammer claimed that a State Department email, which passed along a report from Embassy Tripoli that Ansar al-Sharia had claimed responsibility for the attack on Facebook and Twitter, proved that the White House knew of terrorist connections to the attack almost immediately. Charles Krauthammer stated, "This is really a journalistic scandal. I mean, the fact there was not a word about any of this in the Times or the Posttoday."

Conservative pundit Jonah Goldberg of the *National Review* stated that on NBC's *Meet the Press*, host David Gregory changed the subject when a guest raised the subject of the Benghazi attack, saying, "Let's get to Libya a little bit later," but never returned to the subject.

On November 26, 2012, journalist Tom Ricks went on Fox News' *Happening Now* with Jon Scott to discuss the attack. While being interviewed on Fox News by Jon Scott, Ricks accused Fox News of being "extremely political" in its coverage of the attack and said that "Fox was operating as a wing of the Republican Party." Ricks accused the network of covering the story more than it needed to be. The interview was cut short and Ricks and the interview was not mentioned or covered by Fox News again. Fox News was subsequently criticized for cutting the interview short. In an interview with the Associated Press, Fox News' White House correspondent Ed Henry suggested that he thought Benghazi was being covered too much by the network. Henry said, "We've had the proper emphasis, but I would not be so deluded to say that some of our shows, some of our commentators, have covered it more than it needed to be covered."

A CNN/ORC poll published June 17, 2014 states that 61% of Americans are not satisfied with the Obama administrations handling of the situation, but are split 48% to 44% on whether Republicans have been too aggressive in the hearings.

Investigation

Several official investigations have been completed, are ongoing, or are under consideration. Investigative reporting has also discovered new information about the Obama administration's handling of the aftermath of the attack.

Federal Bureau of Investigation

The FBI opened its investigation soon after the attack and it remains ongoing. No arrests have been made. On May 2, 2013, the FBI released photos of three men from the Benghazi attack site, asking for help from the public in identifying the individuals.

Senate Select Committee on Intelligence

The U.S. Senate Select Committee on Intelligence delivered their bipartisan report on the terrorist attacks on January 15, 2014. The majority of the committee offered the following conclusions:

- The attacks were preventable.
- There were no protests in the area prior to the attack.
- Although the attack did not arise from prior protests, it "did not require significant amounts of preplanning."
- Terrorists who participated in the attacks included members of al-Qa'ida in the Lands of the Islamic Maghreb, Ansar al-Sharia, al-Qaeda in the Arabian Peninsula, and the Mohammad Jamal Network.
- The CIA talking points were flawed but still "painted a mostly accurate picture of the IC's analysis of the Benghazi attacks at that time, in an unclassified form and without compromising the nascent investigation of the attacks."
- In general, the majority concluded "that the interagency coordination process on the talking points followed normal, but rushed coordination procedures and that there were no efforts by

the White House or any other Executive Branch entities to 'cover-up' facts or make alterations for political purposes."

Senators[which?] from the Republican Party offered additional views:

- The U.S. State Department was resistant to cooperating with the Senate investigation.
- The Obama administration manipulated the facts around the attack, with its handling of the attacks having been "a source of confusion" and that the "Administration chose to try to frame the story in a way that minimized any connection to terrorism".

Five House Committees

Five House Committees (Armed Services, Foreign Affairs, Intelligence, Judiciary, and Oversight and Government Reform) initiated their own inquiries soon after the attack. The Republicans on these five House Committees delivered an interim report to the Members of the House Republican Conference on April 23, 2013. The interim report, which contains the conclusions of the Republican majority staff, signed only by the five Republican chairmen of those committees and stated "This staff report has not been officially adopted by the Committee on Armed Services, the Committee on Foreign Affairs, the Committee on the Judiciary, the Committee on Oversight and Government Reform, or the Permanent Select Committee on Intelligence and therefore may not necessarily reflect the views of their Members," was critical of the Obama Administration's actions before, during, and after the attack. Among dozens of findings, the report states that:

- "Senior State Department officials knew that the threat environment in Benghazi was high and that the Benghazi compound was vulnerable and unable to withstand an attack, yet the department continued to systematically withdraw security personnel"

- The " Administration willfully perpetuated a deliberately misleading and incomplete narrative that the attacks evolved from a political demonstration caused by a YouTube video."
- "... after a White House Deputies Meeting on Saturday, September 15, 2012, the Administration altered the talking points to remove references to the likely participation of Islamic extremists in the attacks. The Administration also removed references to the threat of extremists linked to al-Qa'ida in Benghazi and eastern Libya ..."
- "The Administration deflected responsibility by blaming the IC for the information it communicated to the public in both the talking points and the subsequent narrative it perpetuated."

Democrats on the five committees criticized the report, which they said had been written without Democratic input, as a "partisan Republican" work that was "unnecessarily politicizing our national security."

Additional congressional hearings were conducted May 8, 2013 with three "whistleblower" witnesses: Mark Thompson, acting deputy assistant Secretary of State for counterterrorism; Greg Hicks, former deputy chief of mission in Libya; and Eric Nordstrom, former regional security officer in Libya.

On November 7, 2013, Representative David Nunes (R-CA) wrote a letter to House Speaker John Boehner a week ahead of congressional hearing with CIA contractors who were on the ground during the attack. Nunes wrote that if questions remain unanswered or "if some answers differ substantially from the established narrative and timeline of the attack, then it would be warranted to take new measures to complete the investigation and synthesize the information obtained by the Intelligence Committees and other committees investigating the Benghazi attack."

On August 1, 2014 the House Intelligence Committee, has concluded that there was no deliberate wrongdoing by the Obama administration in the 2012 attack on the U.S. Consulate in Benghazi, Libya. Representative Dutch Ruppersberger stated that "the intelligence community warned about an increased environment, but did not have specific tactical warning of an attack before it happened,".

State Department Accountability Review Board

As required by the Omnibus Diplomatic and Antiterrorism Act of 1986, the State Department announced on October 4, 2012 an Accountability Review Board "to examine the facts and circumstances of the attacks." Four members were selected by Clinton and another was selected by Director of National Intelligence James R. Clapper. AmbassadorThomas R. Pickering served as the Chairman, Admiral Michael Mullen served as the Vice Chairman, also serving were Catherine Bertini, Richard Shinnick, and Hugh Turner, who represented the intelligence community.

The investigation report was released December 20, 2012. It was seen as a sharp criticism of State Department officials in Washington for ignoring requests for more guards and safety upgrades, and for failing to adapt security procedures to a deteriorating security environment. "Systemic failures and leadership and management deficiencies at senior levels within two bureaus of the State Department ... resulted in a special mission security posture that was inadequate for Benghazi and grossly inadequate to deal with the attack that took place," said the unclassified version of the report. It also blamed too much reliance on local militias who failed to fend off the attackers that evening. The Council on Foreign Relations in an initial report saw it as a refutation to the notion that the Obama administration delayed its response. The report confirmed that, contrary to initial accounts, there was no protest outside the consulate. It placed responsibility for the incident solely upon the attackers, deemed as terrorists.

Senate Committee on Homeland Security and Governmental Affairs

Homeland Security and Governmental Affairs Committee Chairman Joe Lieberman (ID-CT) and Ranking Member Susan Collins (R-ME) opened an investigation in mid October 2012. Their final report was delivered December 31, 2012. According to the report, "there was a high risk of a 'significant' terrorist attack on U.S. employees and facilities in Benghazi in the months before the September 11, 2012, assault on the Mission, and the State Department failed to take adequate steps to reduce the Mission's vulnerability."

House Select Committee

Main article: United States House Select Committee on Events Surrounding the 2012 Terrorist Attack in Benghazi

In May 2014, House Speaker John Boehner announced a House select committee would be formed to further investigate the attacks in light of State Department documents released on April 29, 2014, to Judicial Watch, a conservative government watchdog group. These documents, including a cache of previously unreleased emails "that House panels had been unable to receive even after issuing a subpoena," were obtained by Judicial Watch under the Freedom of Information Act (FOIA): one document in particular, an email written by a White House adviser, has been labeled by conservatives as a "smoking gun". The House voted May 8, 2014 to establish the United States House Select Committee on Events Surrounding the 2012 Terrorist Attack in Benghazi, voting 232-186 — 225 Republicans and 7 Democrats in favor, 186 Democrats voting against. The Democratic National Committee sent out a statement describing the committee as a "ploy" and "political stunt."

On August 1, 2014 the House Intelligence Committee, led by Republicans, concluded that there was no deliberate wrongdoing by the Obama administration in the 2012 attack on the U.S. Consulate in Benghazi, and that news briefing given by the administration reflected the conflicting intelligence assessments in the days immediately following the crisis.

Investigative reporting and opinion commentary

Armed forces attacked the U.S. consulate during a protest against an anti-Islamist film. Numerous eyewitnesses reported that the attackers said they were reacting to the filmInnocence of Muslims. A Reuters reporter, Hadeel Al-Shalchi, after speaking with authorities, stated: *"There was definitely a protest planned around the consulate to mimic what happened in Egypt. Security even told me that, you know, people who were sympathetic with the cause from the security may have even allowed, you know, people to riot very close to the consulate"*. David D. Kirkpatrick and Suliman Ali Zway of The New York Times reported that there was no peaceful demonstration according to witnesses. A militant organization known as Ansar al-Shariah told people on the scene that they were upset over the video.

On May 3, 2013, Stephen Hayes wrote in *The Weekly Standard* that "senior Obama administration officials knowingly misled the country about what had happened in the days following the assaults." Hayes said that there was a flurry of revisions made to the talking points in the days before Susan Rice, U.S. ambassador to the United Nations, appeared on five Sunday television talk shows. Included in the cuts were references to "Islamic extremists," reminders of warnings about al Qaeda in Libya, a reference to "jihadists" in Cairo, the mention of possible surveillance of the facility in Benghazi, and the report of five previous attacks on foreign interests.

On May 10, 2013, ABC News' Jonathan Karl reported that Stephen Hayes had "obtained 12 different versions of the talking points that show they were extensively edited as they evolved from the drafts first written entirely by the CIA to the final version distributed to Congress and to U.S. Ambassador to the U.N. Susan Rice before she appeared on five talk shows." The changes made to the talking points, according to the report, appear to directly contradict what White House Press Secretary Jay Carney said about them in November 2012. Afterwards, Carney stated the reports did not contradict what he said and that it was the CIA's task to review the talking points. The White House then released copies of various emails that were sent to various administration officials shortly after the attack took place to prove that there was no cover up. On the May 12 episode of ABC News This Week, Karl said that when then-CIA Director David Petraeus saw the final talking points the Saturday before Rice went on the Sunday talk shows he said they were "essentially useless". Karl went on to quote from an e-mail in which Petraeus said of the talking points: "I would just as soon not use them, but it's their call."

Research by other media outlets later proved that Karl's report was inaccurate, as his sources had twisted what was written in the documents. On the May 19 episode of ABC News This Week, Karl announced he regretted reporting the inaccuracy and acknowledged that he exaggerated the words Obama speechwriter Ben Rhodes had written in one of emails cited in the documents. Memos written by State Department spokeswoman Victoria Nuland also revealed that she made the revisions because they "could be abused by members to beat up the State Department for not paying attention to warnings." On July 11, Nuland, who was nominated by Obama to be the top US envoy to Europe, told various members of the Senate Foreign Relations Committee during a confirmation hearing that she had made the revisions and that she had feared Republicans in Congress would politicize the original memos and present a false impression that various top US State Department officials, including then-Secretary of State Hillary Clinton, had covered-up information about the attack.

In August 2013, it was reported by Drew Griffin and Kathleen Johnston of CNN that dozens of CIA operatives were on the ground in Benghazi on the night of the attack. Their sources say 35 people were on the ground in Benghazi the night of attack, and 21 of those worked in the annex building. They further reported that according to their sources the agency was going to great lengths to keep what they were doing a secret, including polygraphing some of the survivors monthly in order to find out if they were talking to the media or Congress. The actions of the CIA were described as pure intimidation, with any leak risking the loss of a career. Former CIA agent Robert Baer described the frequency of the polygraphs as rare.

A six-part report on an investigation by the *New York Times* on the attack was published on the Times website on 28 December 2013. Based on "months of investigation" and "extensive interviews with Libyans in Benghazi who had direct knowledge of the attack there and its context", the investigation found "no evidence that Al Qaeda or other international terrorist groups" had any role in the assault, but that that the attackers included militias that "benefited directly from NATO's extensive air power and logistics support" overthrowing Colonel Qaddafi, and whom the Americans "had taken for allies". It found that the US compound "had been under surveillance at least 12 hours before the assault started", but that the attack also had "spontaneous elements".

Anger at the video [*Innocence of Muslims*] motivated the initial attack. Dozens of people joined in, some of them provoked by the video and others responding to fast-spreading false rumors that guards inside the American compound had shot Libyan protesters. Looters and arsonists, without any sign of a plan, were the ones who ravaged the compound after the initial attack, according to more than a dozen Libyan witnesses as well as many American officials who have viewed the footage from security cameras.

In the following weeks, several U.S. lawmakers (both Democrats and Republicans), publicly stated that "the intelligence indicates that al Qaeda was involved."

FOIA Requests

Freedom of Information Act requests have been made since the attack. The conservative foundation Judicial Watch filed a FOIA request to the Department of State on December 19, 2012. An acknowledgement of the request was received by Judicial Watch on January 4, 2013. When the State Department failed to respond to the request by February 4, 2013, Judicial Watch filed a lawsuit, which resulted in seven photographs being delivered on June 6, 2013. Three of the photographs show Arabic-language spray paint graffiti. According to preliminary translations provided to the U.K. MailOnline by the Investigative Project on Terrorism, the graffiti likely reads "Thrones of Hamzaln"; "Allah-u Akbar" ("God is Great"); and "Unity of ranks".

On May 30, 2013 it was reported that the Republican National Committee filed a FOIA for "any and all emails or other documents containing the terms 'Libya' and/or 'Benghazi' dated between September 11, 2012 and November 7, 2012 directed from or to U.S. Department of State employees originating from, or addressed to, persons whose email addresses end in either 'barackobama.com' or 'dnc.org.'"

On April 18, 2014, the conservative group Judicial Watch released more than 100 pages of documents obtained through a FOIA lawsuit.

One email, dated September 14, 2012, with Subject: "RE PREP CALL with Susan", was from deputy national security advisor for strategic communications Rhodes states:

"Goals: ...To underscore that these protests are rooted in an Internet video, and not a broader failure of policy..."

According to the Wall Street Journal, the email was written to prepare U.S. Ambassador to the U.N. Susan Rice for her appearances on Sunday news shows two days later, and it "sets out the Administration's view of the cause of the Benghazi attacks".

John Dickerson of Slate says the email refers to the worldwide protests to Innocence of Muslims and not the Benghazi attack.

References

1. *b c* Robertson, Nic; Cruickshank, Paul; Lister, Tim (September 13, 2012). "Pro-al Qaeda group seen behind deadly Benghazi attack". CNN. Retrieved December 30, 2012.
2. "Libyan storm Ansar Al-Sharia compound in backlash after attack on US Consulate". FoxNews.com. Associated Press. September 21, 2012.
3. *b* Steven Lee Myers, Clinton Suggests Link to Qaeda Offshoot in Deadly Libya Attack *The New York Times* 26 September 2012
4. Suzanne Kelly, Pam Benson and Elise Labott (October 24, 2012). "US Intel believes some Benghazi attackers tied to al Qaeda in Iraq". CNN.
5. *b c d* Paul Cruickshank, Tim Lister, Nic Robertson, and Fran Townsend, "Sources: 3 al Qaeda operatives took part in Benghazi attack" CNN, May 4, 2013.
6. "U.S. Senate Select Committee Review of the Terrorist Attacks on U.S. Diplomatic Facilities in Benghazi, Libya, September 11-12, 2012". January 15, 2014.
7. "Christopher Stevens first American ambassador to be slain on duty since 1979". Boston Globe. September 13, 2013.
8. UPI (2 November 2012). "US officials: CIA ran Benghazi consulate".
9. Aaron Blake (27 January 2014). "Clinton says Benghazi is her biggest regret". Washington Post.
10. *b* Cooper, Helene (September 14, 2012). "Egypt May Be Bigger Concern Than Libya for White House". New York Times.
11. *b c d* "Libya: Islamist militia bases stormed in Benghazi". BBC. September 22, 2012. Retrieved September 22, 2012.
12. *b c d e f* "Angry Libyans Target Militias, Forcing Flight". *The New York Times*. September 22, 2012. Retrieved September 22, 2012.
13. *b* "US won't rule out Islamist militant link to attack on US consulate in Libya". Worldnews.nbcnews.com. September 12, 2012. Retrieved September 12, 2012.
14. "CIA talking points for Susan Rice called Benghazi attack "spontaneously inspired" by protests". CBS News. November 15, 2012.
15.

16. David D. Kirkpatrick (June 17, 2014). "Brazen Figure May Hold Key to Mysteries". NY Times. Retrieved June 21, 2014.

17. David D. Kirkpatrick (October 18, 2012). "Suspect in Libya Attack, in Plain Sight, Scoffs at U.S.". NY Times. Retrieved June 21, 2014.

18. Perez, Evan (August 7, 2013). "First criminal charges filed in Benghazi attack probe". CNN. Retrieved September 5, 2013.

19. *b* "Terrorist Designations of Three Ansar al-Shari'a Organizations and Leaders". U.S. Department of State. January 10, 2014. Retrieved June 19, 2014.

20. John King and Chelsea J. Carter (7 August 2013). "Lawmaker: If CNN can interview suspect in Benghazi attack, why can't FBI?". CNN. Retrieved May 8, 2014.

21. Erik Wemple (3 April 2014). "New York Times stands by Benghazi story". Washington Post. Retrieved May 8, 2014.

22. http://www.washingtonpost.com/world/national-security/us-captured-benghazi-suspect-in-secret-raid/2014/06/17/7ef8746e-f5cf-11e3-a3a5-42be35962a52_story.html?Post+generic=%3Ftid%3Dsm_twitter_washingtonpost

23. *b* Nic Robertson, "Former jihadist at the heart of Libya's revolution" CNN, September 3, 2011

24. Pargeter, Alison. "Islamist Militant Groups in Post-Qadhafi Libya" West Point, February 20, 2013.

25. Risen, James; Mazzetti, Mark; Schmidt, Michael. "U.S.-Approved Arms for Libya Rebels Fell Into Jihadis' Hands" *The New York Times*, December 5, 2012.

26. *b c* Schmitt, Eric; Cooper, Helene; Schmidt, Michael S. "Deadly Attack in Libya Was Major Blow to C.I.A. Efforts" *The New York Times*, September 23, 2012.

27. *b c d e f g h i j k l m* Murphy, Jack and Brandon Webb (2013). *Benghazi: The Definitive report*. New York, NY: HarperCollins Inc. pp. 25–58. ISBN 978-0-06-227691-9.

28. Cox, Carmen. "US Names Chris Stevens Liaison to Libyan Opposition" *ABC News*, March 14, 2011.

29. Ross, Brian; Cole, Matthew. "Nightmare in Libya: Thousands of Surface-to-Air Missiles Unaccounted For" *ABC News*, September 27, 2011.

30. Coughlin, Con. "Will a Middle East awash with weapons be Gaddafi's final legacy?" *The Telegraph*, October 23, 2011.

31. *b c* Griffin, Drew; Johnston, Kathleen. "Exclusive: Dozens of CIA operatives on the ground during Benghazi attack" *CNN*, August 1, 2013.

32. [b] Murphy, Jack. "America's Assassination Program in Libya" SOFREP, August 5, 2013.

33. "Syrian rebels squabble over weapons as biggest shipload arrives from Libya" *The Times*, September 14, 2012

34. Herridge, Catherine; Browne, Pamela. "Was Syrian weapons shipment factor in ambassador's Benghazi visit?" Fox News, October 25, 2012.

35. McElroy, Damien. "CIA 'running arms smuggling team in Benghazi when consulate was attacked'" *The Telegraph*, August 2, 2013.

36. Seymour Hersh. "The Red Line and the Rat Line". Retrieved April 9, 2014.

37. http://intelligence.house.gov/sites/intelligence.house.gov/files/documents/HPSCIBenghaziUpdateJan2014.pdf

38. [b c] http://www.theguardian.com/world/2013/may/08/benghazi-congressional-hearing-live-blog

39. [b c] http://thehill.com/policy/international/300879-benghazi-witness-points-finger-at-clinton-on-lapses-in-security

40. [b] http://www.washingtonpost.com/blogs/right-turn/wp/2013/05/21/clintons-role-in-the-benghazi-fiasco-and-blame-shifting/

41. [b c] pp. 40-1 & 89, http://oversight.house.gov/wp-content/uploads/2014/02/2013-05-08-Ser.-No.-113-30-FC-Benghazi-Exposing-Failure-and-Recognizing-Courage.pdf

42. [b c] Part I @ 1:59 & Part III @ 33:25, http://oversight.house.gov/hearing/benghazi-exposing-failure-and-recognizing-courage/

43. http://politicalticker.blogs.cnn.com/2013/05/08/the-latest-on-benghazi-hearing/

44. http://www.theguardian.com/world/2013/may/08/benghazi-us-officials-blocked-congress-hearing

45. Lake, Eli (2 October 2012). "U.S. Consulate in Benghazi Bombed Twice in Run-up to 9/11 Anniversary". *The Daily Beast*. Retrieved October 2, 2012.

46. "U.S. embassy Tripoli Libya Security Incidents Since June 2011 hosted by ABC News"(PDF). Retrieved May 14, 2013.

47. "ICRC pulls out of parts of Libya". UPI. August 6, 2012. Retrieved October 21, 2012.

48. Stephen, Chris (2012-06-06). "US diplomatic mission bombed in Libya". London: The Guardian. Retrieved September 12, 2012.

49. "US consulate in Libya bombed – video". London: The Guardian. 2012-06-06. Retrieved September 12, 2012.

50. Issa, Darrell; Chaffetz, Jason (October 2, 2012). *Letter to Hillary Clinton* (PDF). House of Representatives Committee on Oversight and Government Reform. Retrieved October 7, 2012.

51. Robertson, Nic; Cruickshank, Paul; Lister, Tim (September 13, 2012). "Pro-al Qaeda group seen behind deadly Benghazi attack". CNN. Retrieved September 13, 2012.

52. Karadsheh, Jomana; Robertson, Nic (June 6, 2012). "U.S. mission in Benghazi attacked to avenge al Qaeda". CNN.

53. McGreal, Chris. Benghazi attack: US officials look for answers over deadly consulate assault *The Guardian* 12 September 2012

54. "British ambassador to Libya escapes uninjured after his convoy is hit by rocket-propelled grenade". London: Daily Mail. June 11, 2012.

55. "British Guns Accounted For After Benghazi Consulate Attack". The Tripoli Post. October 12, 2012.

56. "Middle East and North Africa, Libya". Foreign and Commonwealth Office of the UK. Retrieved October 21, 2012.

57. Duell, Mark (October 11, 2012). "Missing British guns from US consulate in Libya 'could have been seized by extremists' one month after site was destroyed". London: Daily Mail.

58. "More details emerge on U.S. ambassador's last moments". CNN. September 11, 2012.

59. Erik Wemple, CNN vs. the State Department: A long story *The Washington Post media blog* 23 September 2012

60. Nancy Youssef, Ambassador Stevens twice said no to military offers of more security, U.S. officials say *McClatchy News Service Foreign Staff* 14 May 2013

61. "U.S. officer got no reply to requests for more security in Benghazi". Reuters. October 9, 2012.

62. "Secretary of State Hillary Clinton takes "responsibility" for Benghazi attack". CBS News. October 18, 2012.

63.
 [b] http://www.collins.senate.gov/public/_cache/files/81d5e2d9 -cc8d-45af-aa8b-b937c55c7208/Flashing%20Red- HSGAC%20Special%20Report%20final.pdf

64. [b] David Lerman, Ambassador Died in Smoke While Agents Searched for Him*Bloomberg News* 10 October 2012

65. *b c d* Schemm, Paul; Michael, Maggie (2012-10-27). "Libyan witnesses recount organized Benghazi attack". *Associated Press*. Retrieved October 27, 2012.

66. *b c* Youssef, Nancy A.; Zway, Suliman Ali (September 13, 2012). "No protest before Benghazi attack, wounded Libyan guard says". McClatchy.

67. *b* Klapper, Bradley (2012-10-27). "Timeline of comments on attack on US Consulate".*Associated Press*. Retrieved October 27, 2012.

68. "Libya: 4 arrested over coordinated attack against U.S.". *CBS News*. September 13, 2012. Retrieved November 4, 2012.

69. "TIMELINE OF EVENTS, COMMENTS SURROUNDING BENGHAZI". *Associated Press*. October 19, 2012. Retrieved October 30, 2012.

70. "U.S. studying Benghazi security cam videos". *UPI*. October 9, 2012. Retrieved October 30, 2012.

71. Gertz, Matt. "Four Media Reports From Libya That Linked The Benghazi Attacks To The Anti-Islam Video". Media Matters For America. Retrieved November 21, 2013.

72. *b* "President Obama's Address at 67th U.N. General Assembly". International Information Programs, U.S. Embassy. 2012-09-25. Retrieved October 25, 2012.

73. *b* "Background Briefing on Libya". U.S. Department of State. October 9, 2012. Retrieved October 30, 2012.

74. *b* McLean, Alan; Peçanha, Sergio; Tse, Archie; Waananen, Lisa (October 1, 2012). "The Attack on the American Mission in Benghazi, Libya". *The New York Times*. Retrieved October 28, 2012.

75. Youssef, Nancy A.; Zway, Suliman Ali; Landay, Jonathan S. (September 12, 2012)."Islamists targeted U.S. diplomats with gunfire, RPGs in planned assault, witness says". McClatchy.

76. *b c* Dettmer, Jamie; Dickey, Christopher; Lake, Eli (2012-10-21). "The Truth Behind the Benghazi Attack". The Daily Beast. Retrieved October 29, 2012.

77. *b c d DEPUTY ASSISTANT SECRETARY OF STATE CHARLENE LAMB TESTIMONY BEFORE HOUSE OVERSIGHT COMMITTEE WASHINGTON, DC WEDNESDAY, OCTOBER 10, 2012* (PDF). Committee on Oversight & Government Reform. October 10, 2012. Retrieved October 19, 2012.

78. "REP. JASON CHAFFETZ: AMBASSADOR STEVENS CALLED FOR HELP DURING BENGHAZI ATTACK". *The Blaze*. November 1, 2012.

79.   *b c d* "Timeline: How Benghazi attack, probe unfolded". *CBS News*. November 2, 2012. Retrieved November 4, 2012.

80.   "Top CIA officer in Benghazi delayed response to terrorist attack, US security team members claim". *Fox News*. 6 September 2014. Retrieved 7 September 2014.
Kirkpatrick, David (4 September 2014). "New Book Says C.I.A. Official in Benghazi Held Up Rescue". *New York Times*. Retrieved 7 September 2014.
Szoldra, Paul (4 September 2014). "New Book Claims Top CIA Officer In Benghazi Told Commandos To 'Stand Down' During Attack". *Business Insider*. Retrieved 7 September 2014.
Baier, Bret (September 5, 2014). "Benghazi Bombshell: Security Team Told to 'Stand Down' By CIA Officer". *FoxNewsInsider.com*. Fox News Insider. Retrieved September 10, 2014.
Zuckoff, Mitchell; Annex Security Team (five members) (September 9, 2014). *13 Hours: The Inside Account of What Really Happened In Benghazi*. Hachette Book Group USA.ISBN 9781455582273.

81.   Jessica Chasmar, "Benghazi hero David Ubben still recovering at Walter Reed" The Washington Times, July 25, 2013.

82.   *b* "US envoy dies in Benghazi consulate attack". Al Jazeera English. September 12, 2012. Retrieved September 12, 2012.

83.   David Martin, "U.S. military poised for rescue in Benghazi" *CBS News* 24 October 2012

84.   Entous, Adam; Gorman, Siobhan; Coker, Margaret (November 1, 2012). "CIA Takes Heat for Role in Libya". *The Wall Street Journal*. Retrieved May 13, 2013.

85.   *b* Al-Khalidi, Suleiman (2012-09-17). "Video shows Libyans helping rescue U.S. ambassador after attack". Reuters. Retrieved September 27, 2012.

86.   Abdalgader Fadl (2012-09-16). "بنغازي اهل ومحاولت الامريكي السفير موته قبل انقاذه." YouTube. Retrieved September 27, 2012.

87.   "Travel Warning – Libya". U.S. Embassy in Tripoli, Libya. 2012-09-12. Retrieved May 13, 2013.

88.   "President Obama on the Attack in Benghazi". International Information Programs, U.S. Embassy. 2012-09-12. Retrieved October 3, 2012.

89.   Parkinson, John. "Diplomat: Ambassador in Benghazi Said, 'We're Under Attack'" ABC News, May 8, 2013.

90. Michael, Maggie (2012-09-17). "Video shows Libyans trying to save U.S. ambassador". Associated Press. Retrieved May 22, 2013.

91. "US ambassador killed in Libya attack: Chris Stevens 'given CPR for 90 minutes', says Benghazi doctor". London: The Daily Telegraph. September 13, 2012.

92. [b] Baker, Peter; Kirkpatrick, David D. (September 14, 2012). "Diplomats' Bodies Return to U.S., and Libyan Guards Recount Deadly Riot". *The New York Times*. Retrieved November 4, 2012.

93. Wemple, Erik (November 16, 2012). "Fox News mangled huge Benghazi story". *media blog*. The Washington Post.

94. Griffin, Jennifer (July 26, 2013). "Who was Glen Doherty? Details emerge on former SEAL's final actions in Benghazi". Fox News.

95. Jennifer Griffin, US military's response questioned in wake *FOX News* 24 October 2012

96. Dad of US bodyguard 'blown up twice' in Benghazi says State Department should admit mistakes *NBC News* 4 October 2012

97. "Benghazi timeline: How the attack unfolded". CBS News. November 2, 2012.

98. Sengupta, Kim (September 14, 2012). "Revealed: inside story of US envoy's assassination". *The Independent* (London).

99. "Statement on the Death of American Personnel in Benghazi, Libya". Department of State. September 12, 2012. Retrieved September 12, 2012.

100. Blake, Aaron (27 January 2014). "Clinton says Benghazi is her biggest regret". Washington Post.

101. Hillary Rodham Clinton, Secretary of State. "Statement on the Deaths of Tyrone S. Woods and Glen A. Doherty in Benghazi, Libya (September 13, 2012)". U.S. Department of State. Retrieved September 20, 2012.

102. [b] "Clinton Recognizes Victims of Benghazi Attacks". State Department's Bureau of International Information Programs (IIP). 2012-09-14. Retrieved October 15, 2012.

103. "Former Navy SEALs identified as consulate attack victims". Fox News. September 14, 2012. Retrieved September 13, 2012.

104. Baker, Debbi (September 13, 2012). "Two ex-SEALs from SD killed in Libya". U-T San Diego.

105. Kirkpatrick, David D.; Meyers, Steven Lee (September 12, 2012). "Libya Attack Brings Challenges for

U.S.". *The New York Times*. Retrieved May 15, 2013.
Alfitory, Osama (September 12, 2012). "U.S. ambassador Chris Stevens killed in consulate attack in Libya". *Deseret News*. Associated Press. Retrieved May 15, 2013.

106.   "U.S. officials: CIA ran Benghazi consulate". United Press International. November 2, 2012.

107.   Griffin, Jennifer (26 October 2012). "EXCLUSIVE: CIA operators were denied request for help during Benghazi attack, sources say". *Fox News*. Retrieved October 26, 2012.

108.   "No Libyans died in Benghazi attack". Libya Herald. Retrieved September 15, 2012.

109.   "Wounded U.S. Diplomats Treated In Germany". Huffington Post. September 13, 2012. Retrieved September 13, 2012.

110.   [b] [c] Pickering, Mullen, et. al, Accountability Review Board report on Benghazi (Unclassified) U.S. Department of State. December 18, 2012.

111.   "State: Only four people wounded at Benghazi". The Hill. March 15, 2013. Retrieved September 12, 2013.

112.   "Exclusive: Dozens of CIA operatives on the ground during Benghazi attack". CNN. August 1, 2013. Retrieved September 12, 2013.

113.   [b] "U-T's 2012 Persons of the Year: They died defending us all". *San Diego Union Tribune*. 31 December 2012. Retrieved January 20, 2013.

114.   [b] Ellement, John R. (September 13, 2012). "Winchester native among victims of Libya attack". *The Boston Globe*. Retrieved September 13, 2012.

115.   Stout, Matt (September 13, 2012). "Family of Winchester man killed in Libya: 'He's a hero'". *Boston Herald*. Retrieved September 13, 2012.

116.   Vogel, Steve (September 14, 2012). "Glen Doherty, 42, killed in U.S. Consulate attack in Benghazi". *Washington Post*. Retrieved January 30, 2013.

117.   Ferran, Lee (September 13, 2012). "American Killed in Libya Was on Intel Mission to Track Weapons". ABC News.

118.   [b] Stone, Andrea (September 13, 2012). "Glen Doherty, Security Officer Killed In Libya Attack, Fought Religious Proselytizing In Military". *The Huffington Post*. Retrieved September 13, 2012.

119.   Webb, Brandon; Doherty, Glen (2010). *The 21st-Century Sniper: A Complete Practical Guide*. Skyhorse

Publishing. p. 242. ISBN 978-1-61608-001-3. Retrieved January 26, 2013.

120. Funeral service for Doherty, necn.com. September 19, 2012.
"Funeral In Winchester For Ex-Navy SEAL Killed In Libya Attack". CBS Radio Inc. Associated Press. 19 September 2012. Retrieved March 17, 2013.
Webb, Brandon (21 September 2012). "A Letter to My Friend Glen Doherty". *New York Times*. Retrieved March 17, 2013.
Powers, Martine (19 September 2012). "Winchester pays its respects to former Navy SEAL killed in Libya attack". *Boston Globe*. Retrieved March 17, 2013.

121. "Events and Fundraising". Glen Doherty Memorial Foundation. Retrieved October 18, 2012.

122. Steele, Jeanette (2012-10-12). "Remembering a fallen warrior, on his terms". U-T San Diego. Retrieved October 19, 2012.

123. [b] Pamplin Media Group (September 13, 2012). "OCHS grad among the dead in Libya consulate attack". *Portland Tribune*. Retrieved September 20, 2012.

124. [b] [c] "Benghazi hero laid to rest; chaplains comfort families". Baptist Press. 2012-10-05. Retrieved October 15, 2012.

125. "U.S. officials clarify administration description of two heroes in Libya attack". Washington Guardian. 2012-09-19. Retrieved October 15, 2012.

126. "2 US victims in Libya attacks former SEALs from CA". Boston.com. Associated Press. September 14, 2012. Retrieved September 20, 2012.[dead link]

127. UPI (2 November 2012). "US officials: CIA ran Benghazi consulate". Retrieved 8 May 2014.

128. Eric Schmitt (1 November 2012). "C.I.A. Played Major Role Fighting Militants in Libya Attack". Retrieved May 8, 2014.

129. [b] "Tyrone S. Woods: The Professional". *The Oregonian*. September 14, 2012. Retrieved September 20, 2012.

130. Winter, Michael (September 14, 2012). "Ex-SEAL killed in Libya 'thrived on adrenaline, danger'". *USA Today*. Retrieved September 20, 2012.

131. Spitaleri, Ellen (18 October 2012). "Woods' sacrifice honored at OCHS assembly".*Portland Tribune*. Retrieved July 15, 2013.

132.   [b] Winter, Michael (September 14, 2012). "Ex-SEAL killed in Libya 'thrived on adrenaline, danger'". *USA Today*. Retrieved October 22, 2012.

133.   "DCPD-201200719 - REMARKS AT A TRANSFER OF REMAINS CEREMONY FOR THE VICTIMS OF THE ATTACK ON THE U.S. MISSION IN BENGHAZI, LIBYA". U.S. Government Printing Office. 14 September 2012. Retrieved July 15, 2013. "The President spoke at 2:46 p.m. at Joint Base Andrews, MD. In his remarks, he referred to Dorothy Narvaez-Woods, wife, Tyrone Jr. and Hunter, sons, and Kai, daughter, of Tyrone S. Woods, security officer, Department of State; and Heather Smith, wife of Sean P. Smith, foreign service officer, Department of State, and their children Samantha and Nathan."
Pratt, Timothy (September 14, 2012). "SEAL Veteran With Zest for Adrenaline". *New York Times*. Retrieved July 15, 2013. "Mr. Woods had recently moved from La Jolla, Calif., with his wife, Dorothy, and their infant son, Kai, to a quiet suburban cul-de-sac in Henderson, Nev., less than 10 miles from the Las Vegas Strip. He is also survived by two teenage sons from his marriage to Ms. So, Tyrone Jr. and Hunter."

134.   "SEAL from Ore. killed in Libya buried Thurs.". *KGW*. 20 September 2012. Retrieved March 17, 2013.
SEAL Killed In Libya Buried At Fort Rosecrans. Baltimore Sun. Retrieved March 17, 2013.
CPO Tyrone Snowden Woods, Sr at *Find a Grave*

135.   Paul Cruickshank, "Analysts search for clues in al-Zawahiri remarks on Benghazi" CNN, November 12, 2012.

136.   Paul Cruickshank, Tim Lister and Nic Robertson, "Phone call links Benghazi attack to al Qaeda commander" CNN, March 5, 2013.

137.   "Terrorist Designations of Ansar al-Sharia as an Alias for Al-Qaida in the Arabian Peninsula". *Media Note*. Office of the Spokesperson, U.S. Department of State. October 4, 2012. Retrieved February 7, 2013.

138.   [b] David D. Kirkpatrick, Attack by Fringe Group Highlights the Problem of Libya's Militias *The New York Times* 15 September 2012

139.   [b] David D. Kirkpatrick, Election-Year Stakes Overshadow Nuances of Libya Investigation *The New York Times* 16 October 2012

140.   David Kirkpatrick, "Suspect in Libya Attack, in Plain Sight, Scoffs at U.S." The New York Times, October 18, 2012.

141.		*b* Foster, Peter; Spencer, Richard (September 13, 2012). "US ambassador killed in Libya: investigators probe whether Benghazi assault was planned". *The Daily Telegraph*(London). Retrieved December 30, 2012.

142.		*b* Goodman, Alana (September 13, 2012). "Libya Attack Pre-Planned By Terror Group?". Commentary. Retrieved May 13, 2013.

143.		Wehrey, Frederic (September 12, 2012). "The Wrath of Libya's Salafis". *Sada*. Retrieved December 30, 2012.

144.		Lynch, Sara; Dorell, Oren (September 12, 2012). "Deadly embassy attacks were days in the making". *USA Today*. Retrieved December 30, 2012.

145.		*b* Bell, Larry (December 2, 2012). "Muslim Brotherhood Fox Was Hired To Protect Our Benghazi Consulate Henhouse - Interview". *Forbes*. Retrieved December 30, 2012.

146.		*CNN*, September 13, 2012.

147.		"Obama: U.S. consulate attack in Libya not an act of war". World Wide Pants. September 19, 2012. Retrieved December 18, 2012.

148.		"Remarks by the President at Univision Town Hall with Jorge Ramos and Maria Elena Salinas". White House. September 20, 2012. Retrieved December 18, 2012.

149.		Elise Labott, "Report on Benghazi attack cites 'systemic failures'" CNN, December 19, 2012.

150.		"Benghazi attack suspect arrested in Tunisia; AP reports 2nd suspect killed in Egypt"CBS News, October 24, 2012

151.		"Benghazi suspect Ali Harzi released by Tunisia for lack of evidence, lawyer says" CBS News, January 8, 2013.

152.		"Egypt identifies Benghazi attack suspect killed in Cairo" CBS News, October 25, 2012

153.		*b* Thomas Joscelyn, "Video reportedly shows key suspect from Benghazi attack" The Long War Journal, October 31, 2012.

154.		*b c* Sioban Gorman, "Egyptians Detain Suspected Terrorist Ringleader" *The Wall Street Journal*, December 7, 2012.

155.		U.S. Department of State (October 7, 2013). "Terrorist Designations of the Muhammad Jamal Network and Muhammad Jamal". U.S. Department of State. Retrieved January 4, 2014.

156.		United Nations Security Council (October 21, 2013). "Security Council Committee pursuant to resolutions

1267 (1999) and 1989 (2011) concerning Al-Qaida and associated individuals and entities". United Nations Security Council. Retrieved January 4, 2014.

157.   Paul Cruickshank. Susan Candiotti and Tim Lister, "Sources: Benghazi suspect detained in Libya" CNN, March 14, 2013.

158.   Bill Gertz, "Benghazi attack suspect walks: Libyans release key player in consulate ambush" The Washington Times, June 27, 2013.

159.   http://www.cnn.com/2014/07/14/world/africa/libya-benghazi-suspect-dead/

160.   "Statement regarding the events at US Consulate in Benghazi" (in Arabic). Libyan Prime Minister's Office. September 12, 2012. Retrieved September 12, 2012.

161.   "US ambassador, consul among 4 killed in militia attack on Benghazi consulate". *Russia Today*. September 12, 2012. Retrieved September 12, 2012.

162.   Testa, Jessica (September 12, 2012). "15 Photos Of Libyans Apologizing To Americans" (photographs). *BuzzFeed.com.*(Additional such photographs.)

163.   [b] Worth, Robert F. (September 12, 2012). "Struggle for Ideological Upper Hand in Muslim World Seen as Factor in Attacks". New York Times.

164.   Robin Banerji, "Did Ansar al-Sharia carry out Libya attack?" BBC, September 12, 2012.

165.   [b] Eugene Kiely, "Benghazi Timeline" FactCheck, October 26, 2012.

166.   "Remarks at Reception Marking Eid ul-Fitr". U.S. Department of State. September 13, 2012.

167.   Armbruster, Ben (September 12, 2012). "Clinton: Libya Attacks By A 'Savage Group,' Not Libyan Government Or Its People". *ThinkProgress*. Retrieved September 13, 2012.

168.   Loschky, Jay (August 18, 2012). "Opinion Briefing: Libyans Eye New Relations With the West". Gallup World Polling.

169.   Murphy, Dan (December 26, 2011). "Eastern Libya poll indicates political Islam will closely follow democracy". Christian Science Monitor.

170.   "Survey of Public Opinion in Eastern Libya". International Republican Institute. Retrieved May 22, 2013.

171.   "Belated Response From Egypt". New York Times. September 14, 2012.

172.   Bob Schieffer, ""Face the Nation" transcripts, September 16, 2012: Libyan Pres. Magariaf, Amb. Rice and Sen. McCain" CBS News, September 16, 2012.

173.   Leila Fadel, "Consulate Attack Preplanned, Libya's President Says" NPR, September 16, 2012.

174.   [b c] "Protesting Libyans storm militant compound in backlash against armed groups". NBC. Retrieved September 24, 2012.

175.   [b c d e] Urquhart, Conal (September 22, 2012). "Libyan protesters force Islamist militia out of Benghazi". London: Guardian. Retrieved September 23, 2012.

176.   "UPDATE 3-Libyan Islamist militia swept out of Benghazi bases". *Reuters*. September 22, 2012. Retrieved September 22, 2012.

177.   [b c] Osama Alfitory (24 September 2012). "Libya orders militias to operate under government control or disband". Denver Post.

178.   [b c d e] "Libyan forces raid militia outposts". Al Jazeera. 23 September 2012.

179.   [b] "Disbanding Libya's militias". Al Jazeera. 24 September 2012.

180.   Karadsheh, Jomana (24 September 2012). "Libyan troops raid rogue brigade's base". CNN.

181.   [b] "Libya's army evicts unauthorized militias". CNN. 25 September 2012.

182.   "Hundreds of Libyans hand over their weapons". USA Today. 29 September 2012.

183.   "Libyan militias amass weapons as rivalries surface". The National. 23 September 2012.

184.   Compton, Matt (September 12, 2012). "President Obama Discusses the Attack in Benghazi, Libya". The White House. Retrieved September 14, 2012.

185.   [b c d e] "Remarks by the President on the Death of U.S. Embassy Staff in Libya". White House. September 12, 2012. Retrieved September 22, 2012.

186.   "US Marine anti-terrorism team heads to Libya: official". AFP. September 12, 2012. Retrieved September 12, 2012.

187.   [b] "U.S. launching apparent terrorist hunt in Libya". *CBS News*. September 13, 2012.

188.   Spetalnick, Matt; Hadeel Al Shalchi (September 12, 2012). "Obama vows to track down ambassador's killers". *Reuters*. Retrieved November 5, 2012.

189.   Remarks on the Deaths of American Personnel in Benghazi, Libya, Hillary Rodham Clinton, U.S. Department of State, September 12, 2012

190.   Solomon, John (September 12, 2012). "Years of warning about embassy security preceded Libya attack". *Washington Guardian*. Retrieved November 5, 2012.

191.   "U.S. vows to hunt down perpetrators of Benghazi attack". *CNN*. September 12, 2012. Retrieved November 6, 2012.

192.   "U.S. struggles to determine whether Libya attack was planned". *CNN*. September 13, 2012. Retrieved September 13, 2012.

193.   "Remarks by the President in Golden, CO". The White House. Sep 13, 2012. Retrieved October 18, 2012.

194.   "Press Briefing by Press Secretary Jay Carney, 9/14/2012". The White House. September 14, 2012. Retrieved October 18, 2012.

195.   Remarks at the Transfer of Remains Ceremony to Honor Those Lost in Attacks in Benghazi, Libya, Hillary Rodham Clinton, September 14, 2012

196.   Schmitt, Eric (October 21, 2012). "Explanation for Benghazi Attack Under Scrutiny". *The New York Times*. Retrieved October 27, 2012.(login required)

197.   The Benghazi Talking Points *The New York Times* 28 November 2012

198.   ""Face the Nation" transcripts, September 16, 2012: Libyan Pres. Magariaf, Amb. Rice and Sen. McCain". CBS News. September 16, 2012. Retrieved September 23, 2012.

199.   "Ambassador Susan Rice: Libya Attack Not Premeditated". ABC News. September 16, 2012. Retrieved September 23, 2012.

200.   "Ambassador Rice spends Sunday reinforcing White House position that Middle East violence was 'spontaneous'". Fox News Channel. September 16, 2012. Retrieved September 23, 2012.

201.   "Transcripts, State of the Union with Candy Crowley, interview with Susan Rice". CNN. September 16, 2012. Retrieved September 23, 2012.

202.   "September 16: Benjamin Netanyahu, Susan Rice, Keith Ellison, Peter King, Bob Woodward, Jeffrey Goldberg,". NBC News. September 16, 2012. Retrieved September 23, 2012.

203.   "Press Briefing by Press Secretary Jay Carney, 9/18/2012". September 18, 2012. Retrieved October 18, 2012.

204.   Press Gaggle by Press Secretary Jay Carney en route Miami, FL, 9/20/2012, White House, October 20, 2012

205.   "As Carney labels Libya strike terrorism, Obama continues to incorrectly cite anti-Islam film". *Fox News*. September 20, 2012.

206.   "Obama's Responses To Libya Questions At Univision Forum Contradicted By Reports Of The Attack". *Media Ite*. September 20, 2012.

207.   "Obama pressed on failures at Univision forum". *Politico*. September 20, 2012.

208.   Parsons, Christi (September 20, 2012). "Obama defends embassy security during Univision town hall". *Los Angeles Times*.

209.   "Univision's Town Hall Meeting With President Obama". *Real Clear Politics*. September 20, 2012.

210.   "Anti-film ads in Pakistan feature Obama, Clinton". CBS News. September 24, 2012. Retrieved June 19, 2014.

211.   "Transcript: President Obama Talks to the U.N. about Mideast Peace, Iran". September 27, 2012. Retrieved October 12, 2012.

212.   "Remarks by the President to the UN General Assembly". *Office of the Press Secretary*. White House. 25 September 2012. Retrieved June 3, 2013.

213.   "Transcript: Obama address to U.N. General Assembly". *Fox News*. 25 September 2012. Retrieved June 3, 2013.

214.   "Producer of anti-Islam film arrested, ordered held without bail". *CNN*. 28 September 2012. Retrieved May 30, 2014.

215.   *Statement by the Director of Public Affairs for the Director of National Intelligence, Shawn Turner, on the intelligence related to the terrorist attack on the U.S. Consulate in Benghazi, Libya* (PDF). Office of the Director of National Intelligence. September 28, 2012. Retrieved October 13, 2012.

216.   "FBI came to Benghazi and left in past 24 hours". *Associated Press*. October 4, 2012. Retrieved May 22, 2013.

217.   "Whistle-blower: Botched talking points hurt FBI probe of Benghazi attack". *Fox News*. 8 May 2013. Retrieved May 9, 2013.

"The latest on Benghazi hearing". *CNN*. May 8, 2013. Retrieved June 3, 2013.

218.　　　"Hillary Clinton Benghazi Testimony Postponed After Secretary Of State Sustains Concussion". Huffington Post. December 15, 2012.

219.　　　"Rep. Allen West accuses Hillary Clinton of faking concussion to avoid Benghazi testimony". New York Daily News. December 20, 2012.

220.

221.　　　"In Context: Hillary Clinton's 'What difference does it make' comment". Tampa Bay Times. May 7, 2013.

222.　　　Schmitt, Eric (October 15, 2012). "U.S. to Help Create an Elite Libyan Force to Combat Islamic Extremists". *New York Times*.

223.　　　Walker, Mark (March 15, 2013). "Medal Proposed for Ex-SEALs". *San Diego Union Tribune*. Retrieved March 15, 2013.
Herb, Jeremy (March 15, 2013). "Hunter wants Congressional medal awarded to slain Benghazi SEALs". *The Hill*. Retrieved March 15, 2013.
"H.R.1186 - To posthumously award the Congressional Gold Medal to each of Glen Doherty and Tyrone Woods in recognition of their contributions to the Nation.". *Congress.gov*. Library of Congress. March 14, 2013. Retrieved March 15, 2013.

224.　　　"H.R. 2848 - All Actions". United States Congress. Retrieved September 30, 2013.

225.　　　"House Report 113-226". United States House Committee on Foreign Affairs. Retrieved September 30, 2013.

226.　　　[b] Sources: 15 days after Benghazi attack, FBI still investigating from afar *CNN* 26 September 2012

227.　　　Green, J.J. (13 September 2012). "Congressman: Consulate attack in Libya was coordinated". *WTOP*. Retrieved November 5, 2012.

228.　　　"Intelligence chairman doubts Libya attack linked to video". CNN. September 23, 2012.

229.　　　Rogin, Josh (September 20, 2012). "Republican senators decry 'useless, worthless' Clinton briefing on Libya attack". Foreign Policy. Retrieved September 22, 2012.

230.　　　Bolton, Alexander (September 22, 2012). "Senate GOP furious newspaper got better briefing on Libya". The Hill. Retrieved September 22, 2012.

231.   "STATE OF THE UNION WITH CANDY CROWLEY, Interview with John McCain; Interview with David Axelrod; Interview with Martin O'Malley, Roy Blunt". *CNN*. September 30, 2012. Retrieved October 15, 2012.

232.   "CNN Fact Check: A day after Libya attack, Obama described it as 'acts of terror'".*CNN*. 17 October 2012. Retrieved July 3, 2013.

233.   Monroe, Bryan (20 October 2012). "The truth about what Candy Crowley said". *CNN*. Retrieved December 3, 2013.

234.   [b] Kesller, Glenn (14 May 2013). "Obama's claim he called Benghazi an 'act of terrorism'". *Washington Post*. Retrieved May 19, 2013.

235.   Kesller, Glenn (1 March 2011). "About the Fact Checker". *Washington Post*. Retrieved July 3, 2013.

236.   ""Face the Nation" transcripts, October 28, 2012: McCain and Emanuel". CBS. October 28, 2012.

237.   "U.S. military poised for rescue in Benghazi". CBS News. Retrieved May 14, 2013.

238.   "Interview with Senator McCain re Benghazi". HughHewitt.com. October 29, 2012. Retrieved January 16, 2014.

239.   "The Benghazi Transcripts: US military woefully unprepared for attack, documents show". Fox News. January 14, 2014. Retrieved May 30, 2014.

240.   Starr, Barbara (April 2, 2013). "After Benghazi, Marines approved for crisis response force". *CNN*. Retrieved April 21, 2013.

241.   "Spain authorizes U.S. rapid reaction force in south". *Army Times* (Gannett Government Media). Associated Press. 19 April 2013. Retrieved April 21, 2013.

242.   Barrett, Wayne (2012-10-22). "Romney Campaign, Media Collude in Unprecedented Politicization of Benghazi Attack". The Nation. Retrieved September 5, 2013.

243.   Miller, Zeke J (2013-05-10). "White House: GOP Focus On Benghazi Tied To Mitt Romney". Time. Retrieved September 5, 2013.

244.   Talev, Margaret (October 15, 2012). "Ambassador's dad says son's death in Libya shouldn't be politicized". Cleveland.com. Retrieved September 5, 2013.

245.   Josh Rogin , "Issa's Benghazi document dump exposes several Libyans working with the U.S." Foreign Policy, October 19, 2012.

246.   ""Gates: Some Benghazi critics have "cartoonish" view of military capability."". Cbsnews.com. Retrieved May 14, 2013.

247.   Saenz, Arlette (May 13, 2013). "President Obama Dismisses Benghazi Criticism as 'Sideshow'". *ABC News*. Retrieved May 19, 2013.
"Obama calls Benghazi controversy a 'sideshow'". *Fox News*. 13 May 2013. Retrieved May 19, 2013.

248.   Schwartz, Ian (2013-07-31). "Carney Identifies Which Scandals Obama Thinks Are Phony: Benghazi And IRS". RealClearPolitics. Retrieved September 5, 2013.

249.   Dinan, Stephen (2 November 2012). "Study: Media accepted Obama version of Benghazi attack". *Washington Times*. Retrieved June 3, 2013.

250.   Wemple, Erik (November 26, 2013). "'60 Minutes' and Benghazi: Five hard realities". The Washington Post. Washington Post.com. Retrieved June 22, 2014.

251.   [b] Pollowitz, Greg (November 6, 2012). "Bret Baier vs. CBS, Obama on Benghazi". National review Online. Retrieved June 21, 2014.

252.   [b] "What President Obama really said in that '60 Minutes' interview about Benghazi".*Fox News*. November 5, 2012.

253.   "Brit Hume: Left-Leaning Media Bias Is Tangible". *CBN News*. October 18, 2012.

254.   "The Rachel Maddow Show". *MSNBC*. September 13, 2012.

255.   "Americans poorly served by media on Iraq, Benghazi". Retrieved June 25, 2014.

256.   "Maddow: U.S. Got the Suspect and 'Benghazi Central' Fox News Doesn't Care?". Retrieved June 25, 2014.

257.   Hosenball, Mark (October 23, 2012). "White House told of militant claim two hours after Libya attack: emails". Reuters. Retrieved June 21, 2013.

258.   Schmitt, Eric (October 23, 2012). "E-Mails Offer Glimpse at What U.S. Knew in First Hours After Attack in Libya". New York Times. Retrieved June 21, 2013.

259.   "Krauthammer: Lack of Benghazi media coverage 'a journalistic scandal'". *The Daily Caller*. October 25, 2012.

260.   "Benghazi: No 'October Surprise'". *National Review*. October 31, 2012.

261.   "October 28: John Kasich, Scott Walker, John Hickenlooper, E.J. Dionne, Rachel Maddow, Carly Fiorina,

David Brooks". MSNBC. October 28, 2012. Retrieved December 18, 2012.

262.   Weinger, Mackenzie (26 November 2012). "Tom Ricks to Fox News: The network operates 'as a wing of the Republican Party'". Politico. Retrieved December 11, 2012.

263.   Wemple, Erik (27 November 2012). "Ricks: Fox doesn't care about story behind Benghazi story". Washington Post. Retrieved December 11, 2012.

264.   Wemple, Erik (6 December 2012). "Does Fox News's Ed Henry agree with Tom Ricks?". Washington Post. Retrieved December 11, 2012.

265.   Bauder, David (6 December 2012). "Ed Henry: Some Fox News Shows Covered Benghazi 'More Than It Needed To Be'". Huffington Post. Retrieved December 11, 2012.

266.   "CNN/ORC Poll: Majority dissatisfied with handling of Benghazi". CNN. June 17, 2014. Retrieved June 17, 2014.

267.   "Images Released in Benghazi Investigation". FBI. May 2, 2013. Retrieved May 7, 2012.

268.   (PDF) ☐Review of the terrorist attacks on U.S. facilities in Benghazi, Libya, September 11-12, 2012 together with additional views☐ (Report). U.S. Senate Select Committee on Intelligence. January 15, 2014. Retrieved January 15, 2014.

269.   Benghazi Report By House Republicans Faults State Department On Libya Security,Huffington Post, 23 April 2013

270.   ᵇ ᶜ "Progress Report on Benghazi Terror Attack Investigation". Committees on Armed Services, Foreign Affairs, Intelligence, Judiciary, and Oversight and Government Reform. April 23, 2013. Retrieved May 7, 2012.

271.   House report on fatal Benghazi attack faults State Department for security, FOX News, 23 April 2013

272.   "Oversight Committee Announces Witnesses for Wednesday Benghazi Hearing". Committee on Oversight & Government Reform. May 8, 2013. Retrieved May 8, 2012. "U.S. Consulate Attack in Benghazi, Libya, Part 1". C-SPAN video library. C-SPAN. 8 May 2013. Retrieved May 10, 2013.

273.   "Congressman: Benghazi questions need answers, or more steps needed". CNN. November 7, 2013. Retrieved November 14, 2013.

274.   Lochhead, Carolyn (August 1, 2014). "House panel: No administration wrongdoing in Benghazi attack". San Francisco Chronicle. Retrieved September 12, 2014.

275.   Walsh, Deirdre (August 6, 2014). "Benghazi probe presses ahead despite new report".CNN. Retrieved August 20, 2014.

276.   "Convening of an Accountability Review Board To Examine the Circumstances Surrounding the Deaths of Personnel Assigned in Support of the U.S. Government Mission to Libya in Benghazi, Libya on September 11, 2012". Federal Register. October 4, 2012. Retrieved October 15, 2012.

277.   Arshad Mohammed, Anna Yukhananov and Tabassum Zakaria Inquiry harshly criticizes State Department over Benghazi attack Reuters. December 18, 2012.

278.   Lake, Eli. In Wake of Benghazi, State Wants $1.3 Billion to Beef Up Security Around the World. The Daily Beast. December 18, 2012.

279.   Hounshell, Blake Benghazi Panel Rebuts Conspiracy Theorists Foreign Policy. December 18, 2012.

280.   Lee, Matthew and Dozier, Kim.Benghazi Attack Report Finds Systematic Management Failures At State Department Led To Inadequate Security. Associated Press viaHuffington Post. December 18, 2012.

281.   "Senators Lieberman, Collins Release Report on Benghazi Security Considerations". U.S. Senate Committee on Homeland Security and Governmental Affairs. December 31, 2012. Retrieved May 7, 2012.

282.   [b] http://www.politico.com/story/2014/05/benghazi-select-committee-john-boehner-eric-cantor-trey-gowdy-house-republicans-106426.html

283.   Wesley Lowery (5 May 2014). "Boehner taps Rep. Trey Gowdy to lead Benghazi select committee". Washington Post. Retrieved May 8, 2014.

284.   http://www.foxnews.com/politics/2014/05/08/house-approves-benghazi-select-committee-probe/

285.   "House votes to establish select committee on Benghazi". Fox News. 8 May 2014. Retrieved May 10, 2014.

286.   "Democrats: Benghazi Investigation Is Just A 'Political Stunt'". Business Insider. May 9, 2014. Retrieved June 17, 2013.

287.   sfchronical.com, August 1, 2014, House panel: No administration wrongdoing in Benghazi attack by Carolyn Lochhead, SF Chronicle: House Panel: No Administration Wrongdoing

288.   Marietta Daily Journal: GOP bury House Benghazi report

289.   "How Benghazi Is Reacting To The Deadly Attacks". *National Public Radio*. September 13, 2012. Retrieved November 21, 2013.

290.   Scott Shane, Clearing the Record About Benghazi *The New York Times* October 18, 2012

291.   "The Benghazi Talking Points: And how they were changed to obscure the truth". The Weekly Standard. May 13, 2013. Retrieved May 13, 2012.

292.   *b c* "Exclusive: Benghazi Talking Points Underwent 12 Revisions, Scrubbed of Terror Reference". ABC News. May 10, 2013. Retrieved May 12, 2012.

293.   "Full Benghazi Talking Points Revisions". May 10, 2013. Retrieved May 12, 2013.

294.   *b c* Fung, Katherine (May 19, 2013). "Jonathan Karl: I 'Regret' Inaccuracies In Benghazi Reporting". *Huffington Post*. Retrieved September 28, 2013.

295.   "Roundtable I: Battle Over Benghazi". ABC News. May 12, 2013. Retrieved May 12, 2013.

296.   Bradley Clapper (July 11, 2013). "Victoria Nuland Answers Benghazi Questions During Senate Confirmation Hearing". Associated Press, Huffington Post. Retrieved September 23, 2013.

297.   *b c* Kirkpatrick, David D.; Suliman Ali Zway; Osama Alfitori; Mayy El Sheikh (December 28, 2013). "A Deadly Mix in Benghazi". *New York Times*. Retrieved December 29, 2013.

298.   "Yes, There IS Evidence Linking al Qaeda to Benghazi". The Daily Beast. December 29, 2013. Retrieved January 14, 2014.

299.   "Feinstein rejects NYT on Benghazi". The Hill. January 14, 2014. Retrieved January 14, 2014.

300.   "Judicial Watch Obtains First Photos from State Department Depicting Aftermath of Benghazi Attack". Judicial Watch. June 21, 2013. Retrieved August 23, 2012.

301.   Martosko, David (June 20, 2013). "'Allah-u-Akbar': State Department unclassifies first official photos from aftermath of Benghazi attack, including jihadi graffiti left behind". London: MailOnline. Retrieved August 23, 2012.

302.   "RNC Files FOIA Request for Benghazi Emails Between State Dept. and Obama 2012 Campaign". Human Events. May 30, 2013. Retrieved August 23, 2012.

303.   "Judicial Watch: Benghazi Documents Point to White House on Misleading Talking Points". Judicial Watch. April 18, 2014. Retrieved April 29, 2014.

304.   http://www.foxnews.com/opinion/2014/04/30/benghazi-emails-obama-white-house-put-politics-ahead-truth/

305.   *Documents obtained through FOIA* by Judicial Watch. Retrieved May 4, 2014.

306.   "The missing Benghazi email". WSJ. 30 April 2014. Retrieved May 28, 2014.

307.   *Lies, Damned Lies, and Garden-Variety Self-Deception* by John Dickerson. Retrieved May 4, 2014.

308.   http://creativecommons.org/licenses/by-sa/3.0/

APPENDIX I

THE SECURITY FAILURES OF BENGHAZI

===

HEARING
before the
COMMITTEE ON OVERSIGHTAND GOVERNMENT REFORM
HOUSE OF REPRESENTATIVES
ONE HUNDRED TWELFTH CONGRES
SSECOND SESSION

_____

OCTOBER 10, 2012

_____

Serial No. 112-193

_____

COMMITTEE ON OVERSIGHT AND GOVERNMENT
REFORM

Wednesday, October 10, 2012

House of Representatives,

Committee on Oversight and Government Reform,
Washington, D.C.

The committee met, pursuant to call, at 12:05 p.m., in Room 2154, Rayburn House Office Building, Hon. Darrell E. Issa presiding.

Present: Representatives Issa, Burton, Jordan, Chaffetz, Lankford, Gosar, Labrador, Meehan, DesJarlais, Gowdy, Ross, Farenthold, Kelly, Cummings, Norton, Kucinich, Lynch, Cooper, Connolly, Davis, and Murphy.

Also Present: Representatives Rohrabacher and Adams.

Staff Present: Ali Ahmad, Communications Adviser; Thomas A. Alexander, Senior Counsel; Brien A. Beattie, Professional Staff Member; Robert Borden, General Counsel; Molly Boyl, Parliamentarian; Lawrence J. Brady, Staff Director; Sharon Casey, Senior Assistant Clerk; John Cuaderes, Deputy Staff Director; Adam P. Fromm, Director of Member Services and Committee Operations; Linda Good, Chief Clerk; Frederick Hill, Director of Communications and Senior Policy Advisor; Mitchell S. Kominsky, Counsel; Jim Lewis, Senior Policy Advisor; Mark D. Marin, Director of Oversight; Rafael Maryahin, Counsel; Kevin Corbin, Minority Professional Staff Member; Ashley Etienne, Minority Director of Communications; Susanne Sachsman Grooms, Minority Counsel; Devon Hill, Minority Staff Assistant; Jennifer Hoffman, Minority Press Secretary; Carla Hultberg, Minority Chief Clerk; Peter Kenny, Minority Counsel; Dave Rapallo, Minority Staff Director; Rory Sheehan, Minority New Media Press Secretary; and Carlos Uriarte, Minority Counsel.

Chairman Issa. The committee will come to order. Would you please take your seats?

Perhaps most appropriately today, the Oversight Committee mission statement reads: We exist to secure two fundamental principles. First, that Americans have a right to know that the money Washington takes from them is well spent. And second, Americans deserve an efficient, effective government that works for them.

Our duty on the Oversight and Government Reform Committee is to protect these rights. Our solemn responsibility is to hold government accountable to taxpayers because taxpayers have a right to know what they get from their government. It is our job to work tirelessly, in partnership with citizen watchdogs, to deliver the facts to the American people and bring genuine reform to the Federal bureaucracy. This is the mission of the Government Oversight and Reform Committee.

On September 11th, 2012, four brave Americans serving their country were murdered by terrorists in Benghazi, Libya. Tyrone Woods spent 2 decades as a Navy SEAL, serving multiple tours in Iraq, Afghanistan. Since 2010, he protected the American diplomatic personnel. Tyrone leaves behind a widow and three children.

Glen Doherty, also a former SEAL, and an experienced paramedic, had served his country in both Iraq and Afghanistan. His family and colleagues grieve today for his death.

Sean Smith, a communications specialist, joined the State Department after 6 years in the United States Air Force. Sean leaves behind a widow and two young children.

Ambassador Chris Stevens, a man I had known personally during his tours, U.S. Ambassador to Libya, ventured into a volatile and dangerous situation as Libyans revolted against the long-time Qadhafi regime. He did so because he believed the people of Libya wanted and deserved the same things we have, freedom from tyranny.

We join here today expressing, from this side of the dais, our deepest sympathy for the loss of lives of the families in Libya.Additionally, other Americans were injured in thisterrorist attack, some suffering very serious injuries. I spoketo the father of one American who is presently recovering herein the United States in a military hospital. He hopefully willhave a full recovery, but he has gone through supplementalsurgeries that will require a long period of recuperation andreconstruction.

Yesterday, the State Department began the process of coming clean about what occurred in Benghazi, or at least they issued a broad and definitive statement headed by a gentleman here today, Ambassador Kennedy. They made witnesses available in interviews. They made every effort from what we can tell to ensure that the people we wanted to talk to were available to us.

More importantly, yesterday they held a broad news conference over the phone in which they made it very clear that it had never been the State Department's position, I repeat never been the State Department's position, that in fact, this assault was part of a reaction to a video or the like. This is corroborated by numerous witnesses and whistleblowers. Contrary to early assertions by the administration, let's understand there was no protest. And cameras reveal that. And the State Department, the FBI, and others have that video.

Speaking of video, the one in California, made by an individual and out there for a period of time, also clearly had no direct effect on this attack. In fact, it was September 11th, the 11th anniversary of the greatest terrorist attack in U.S. history in New York, Pennsylvania, and at the Pentagon. It was that anniversary that caused an organization aligned with al Qaeda to attack and kill our personnel.

I deeply, again, appreciate Secretary Clinton's efforts to cooperate with this investigation. She stepped in and instructed her people to cooperate, and they have. Additionally, I have had conversations directly with the Secretary, and I believe that our service together since 2001 in the United States Congress plays no small part in her recognition of the role we serve on both sides of the dome.

Today, however, this hearing has been called for the express purpose of examining security failures that led to the Benghazi tragedy. The safe haven within the compound which some State Department officials seem to think could protect the Benghazi compound's inhabitants did not work, and in retrospect could not be expected to work. The overall level of security at the compound did not meet the threat existent or standards under Inman or any other reasonable assessment for a facility of this sort.

Today's hearing is the result of concerned citizens with direct knowledge of the events in Libya ultimately reaching this committee. As we look back on what occurred, our challenge is to identify things that clearly went wrong, and what the benefit of hindsight will be for the men and women serving at dangerous locations around the world.

Accounts from security officials who were on the ground and documents indicate that they repeatedly warned Washington officials about the dangerous situation in Libya. Instead, however, of moving swiftly to respond to these concerns, Washington officials seemed preoccupied with the concept of normalization.

We will ask our panel here today what normalization means. In accounts we have heard, it included artificial timelines for removing American security personnel, replacing them with local Libyans. These occurred even as training delays and new threats also occurred. This rush toward a reduced presence of U.S. personnel continued even as a bomb blew a 12-foot opening in the wall of this very compound we speak about today. Requests for extensions of more security by the mission in Libya, however, appeared to have often been rejected, or even, more deliberately, officials in Washington told diplomats in Libya not even to make them. Or as we have had in sworn testimony, if you make them they will not be supported.

We know that the tragedy in Benghazi ended as it did. We now know that in fact it was caused by a terrorist attack that was reasonably predictable to eventually happen somewhere in the world, especially on September 11th.

In closing, as Secretary Clinton has empaneled a blue ribbon board to fully investigate what occurred, and this work is important, it is much broader for us and for that panel to take up an additional challenge. There are hundreds and hundreds of facilities similar to this around the world. There are thousands of personnel serving this country who at any time in any country could be a target. Some of those are high risk and obvious, like Libya. Others may be lower risk. This committee is dedicated to ensure that security is taken differently than it was leading up to the events here. We owe it to our Federal employees who put themselves and their families in harm's way around the world.

The history of these panels is in fact that they deliver full and complete results and they pull no punches. Admiral Mullen is no stranger to controversy, and in fact getting to the bottom of it. So I do encourage all to look at the final result of the blue ribbon panel.

But today it is 30 days since the September 11th attack, more or less. It is a long time to wait if you are sitting in Cairo, in Algeria, in Beirut, in Damascus and you don't trust that the security measures you need have occurred. Today we begin the process of saying they must be able to trust because you must be able to assure them that you are doing your work differently than just a short time ago.

Today, we expect full cooperation from our panel. We expect to get to the truth. But it will, in fact, be a much longer time before all the facts are known. We do not intend to flesh out all the facts. We intend today, on a bipartisan basis, to ensure that we begin the confidence building for our men and women serving this country around the world that we will ensure that they be protected and, if anything, protected more than the perceived threat, and never less.

With that, I recognize the ranking member for his opening comments. And then by unanimous consent, one additional, the chairman of the Subcommittee on National Security and his counterpart will be recognized for opening statements. All other members will have 7 days in order to put their opening statements in the record. With that, I recognize Mr. Cummings.

Mr. Cummings. Thank you very much, Mr. Chairman. And let me be very clear. You said that your side of the aisle grieves the loss of our fellow countrymen. It is not just your side of the aisle, Mr. Chairman, it is this side of the aisle and our entire country. We grieve the loss of Ambassador Christopher Stevens, Sean Smith, and Navy SEALs Glen Doherty and Tyrone Woods.

I believe we should conduct a thorough and responsible investigation into the attack on the United States mission in Benghazi. We need to carefully, very carefully investigate allegations that have been made over the past week. And we need to run them to the ground before we jump to conclusions. We should not be about the business of drawing conclusions and then looking for the facts.

Let me start by thanking Secretary Clinton and the State Department for cooperating fully with this committee. They agreed to all of our witness requests. They offered additional witnesses beyond those requested. They promptly organized interviews with department officials. And they have been collecting documents sought by the committee.

Today, there are several specific allegations I would like to ask the witnesses about. For example, Mr. Eric Nordstrom, a former regional secretary officer in Tripoli, he told the committee there should have been five diplomatic security agents in Benghazi. In other interviews we conducted yesterday, we learned that there were, that there were in fact five agents in Benghazi on the day of the attack. Should there have been even more? We will ask him about this. And I hope he will be prepared to answer that, because there has been so many allegations in the press saying that there were not. And we will ask the State Department for its views as well.

Another witness, Colonel Andrew Wood, has said he believes that a military unit stationed in Tripoli should have had its term extended because of security concerns in Libya. Just yesterday, we learned that this team was extended not once, but twice. Should it have been extended a third time? We need to ask. Where else was it needed? And were its functions being fully served by others on the ground by the time it left the country?

We should listen carefully to these and other allegations. We should listen just as carefully to the responses. I am disappointed to say, however, that although the chairman claims we are pursuing this investigation on a ``bipartisan basis,'' that has simply not been the case. For example, the chairman concealed the committee's interactions with Colonel Wood until Friday night, when he appeared on national television. The chairman then refused requests to make Colonel Wood available so we could speak with him, ask him basic questions, and prepare for the hearing. We could not even get a phone number. The chairman has withheld documents that were provided to the committee, which is in violation of the House rules. And he effectively excluded Democrats from a congressional delegation to Libya this past weekend. We were told about the trip less than 24 hours before it was supposed to take place.

It is a shame that they are resorting to such petty abuses in what should be a serious and responsible investigation of this fatal attack. The problem is that these actions deny members of this committee the ability to effectively and efficiently investigate this incident. The members on this side of the aisle are just as concerned as the members on the other side of the aisle. We each represent about 700,000 each people too. We want to make sure that all the questions are answered.

In contrast, on the Senate side, every member of the Foreign Relations Committee, Democrats and Republicans alike, joined in a bipartisan letter to the State Department requesting information on the attack.

So what do we do today? What do we do today? My goal is to try in some way to put the toxic partisanship behind us and focus on the security of our personnel. Every 2 years we put our hands up, as Members of this Congress, and we swear to protect the people of the United States of America. All of us do that. Not just Republicans, not just Democrats, all of us. And those people that we promised to protect are not limited to just the folks that are within our shores and our boundaries of this Nation, but those people who go out and put their lives on the line every day for us in foreign lands.

The chairman has said that our committee will examine not only the Libya attack, but security at outposts across the Middle East. Mr. Chairman, I fully support this effort. And if that is our goal, we have to examine the funding. The fact is that since 2011, the House has cut embassy security by hundreds of millions of dollars below the amounts requested by the President. The House has done that. The Senate restored some of these funds, but the final amounts were still far below the administration's request. And they were far below the levels we enacted in 2010.

Mr. Chairman, I just heard what you said about making sure that we do everything in our power to make sure that this never happens again. And I join you in that statement. And we can do better. I would like to ask the chairman to join me in doing so. Mr. Chairman, I ask you to join me in calling on our leaders in the House to immediately consider a supplemental funding bill to restore funding for embassy security that was cut by the House over the past 2 years.

According to the Joint Committee on Taxation, we could save $2.5 billion per year just by eliminating the tax break for oil companies.

Even Republicans now agree that we should do this, including Governor Romney. We could fully replenish these embassy security accounts with just a fraction of that amount. Restoring our commitment to embassy security could make a real difference for thousands of Americans who serve our country overseas, often in extremely dangerous circumstances, as you, Mr. Chairman, just stated. And I do agree with you, we should act with utmost urgency. Every single moment counts.

From this day forward, it is my hope that our committee will thoroughly investigate this matter in a truly bipartisan manner, because our dedicated Foreign Service personnel and our Nation deserve nothing less.

With that, I yield back.

Chairman Issa. I thank the gentleman. I might note for the record that I said this side of the dais, which is all of us on the dais relative to all of those in the audience.

Mr. Cummings. Mr. Chairman, thank you very much.

Chairman Issa. Thank you. Although you didn't name a particular rule that you say I violated, do you have a rule that you believe I violated?

Mr. Cummings. We will provide you with that. We want to get on with the hearing. But I promise you I will provide you with it.

Chairman Issa. With that, I would ask unanimous consent that our colleagues Mr. Rohrabacher and Ms. Adams be allowed to participate, pursuant to our rules. Without objection, so ordered.

We now recognize the chairman of the Subcommittee on National Security, and the individual who first began this investigation, Mr. Chaffetz.

Mr. Chaffetz. Thank you. Thank you, Mr. Chairman. And I thank all of the members on both sides of the aisle for being here today. I thank the chairman for his tenacity in pursuing this. I believe we have a moral imperative to pursue this. We have four dead Americans. We have others that are critically injured. Our thoughts and prayers on both sides of the aisle are with those people and their families. We cannot thank them enough for their service, their dedication to our Nation. We also thank the people here on this panel for participating, as I know all four of you care deeply about this country.

This is a very serious situation. We have to understand how we got here, because before 9/11, 2012, and after the revolution there in Libya, it was a very tumultuous and difficult situation. I would ask unanimous consent to enter into the record a document that was provided to us by Mr. Eric Nordstrom. It was dated October 1st.

Chairman Issa. Without objection, so ordered.

Mr. Chaffetz. I would like to read, Mr. Chairman, the last paragraph of that statement that he sent to us. There was, again, 230 security incidents in the country of Libya. ``These incidents paint a clear picture that the environment in Libya was fragile at best, and could degrade quickly, certainly not an environment where post should be directed to, quote, 'normalize,' end quote, operations and reduce security resources in accordance with an artificial timetable.''

Of all the things I have seen and read, that to me is one of the most disturbing. And I appreciate the guts of those that stood up and will provide us this information, because it does take guts to do it.

I am going to ask that we have some photos here. We have to understand how we got here. Broad daylight, June of 2012, two-car convoy carrying the British ambassador was ambushed military-style with rocket propelled grenades in Benghazi. Sorry, these pictures seem to be out of order. What you haven't seen before--there we go-- this was an attack literally weeks before what happened in Benghazi.

Next slide, please. And the next. And the next. And the next. These pictures are of an attack that happened in Benghazi. The first was a so-called fish bomb. This is the compound in Benghazi before the attack. Go to the next slide, please. The second bombing was an improvised explosive device that was placed on the north gate, breaching the wall. It was a test by terrorists, and it was successful. And we didn't respond fully and adequately. We didn't acknowledge it. We didn't talk about it. We pretended it didn't happen. It was a terrorist attack on a U.S. asset in Libya and it was never exposed.

We pretended it didn't happen. Well, guess what? The third time the terrorists came to attack us they were even more successful, killing four Americans. I believe personally with more assets, more resources, just meeting the minimum standards, we could have and should have saved the life of Ambassador Stevens and the other people that were there.

Now, this was a massive attack, no doubt about it. We are getting new details. And I believe, Mr. Chairman, the reason we have those details is because of this hearing.

Mysteriously, the State Department decided to give a press briefing last night. We weren't invited. Certain news outlets weren't invited. Any reasonable person looking at the security situation in Libya had to come to the conclusion that it was tumultuous at best. I wish I could tell you everything that I learned. I did go to Libya. I did drop everything. I had the same type of notice that was given to the Democrats. In fact, the State Department sent an attorney to follow me in my every footstep. So to suggest you didn't have an opportunity to go is absolutely wrong. I wish I could share everything that I learned there. But we have to be careful about the sensitive secure information, about sources and methods in a classified setting. I think some of the information that the State Department has shared overstepped some of those bounds. Let us be careful today to not reveal some of that classified information. It has been too hard, too difficult to get basic information. I will tell you, though, that when I was in Libya a good part of the day, never once did a person ever mention a video. Never. And I am fascinated to know and understand from the President of the United States, from the Secretary of State, and from the Ambassador to the United Nations how they can justify that this video caused this attack. It was a terrorist attack. Let's be honest about it.

Mr. Chairman, I appreciate the time. I look forward to this hearing. May God bless those men and women who serve us. I thank you for being here. And let's always remember those who serve this Nation. I yield back.

Chairman Issa. I thank the gentleman. The gentleman is correct, both sides were informed once we had gotten clearance for Libya.

And with that, we recognize the gentlelady from the District of Columbia for a response.

Ms. Norton. Mr. Chairman, the tragic events in Benghazi point up the hazards of serving our country go far beyond the military. I agree with Mr. Chaffetz that perhaps had there been more resources we might have had a different result. But I must note that while the Republican budget increases the budget of the Defense Department, it slashes the budget that would have protected these diplomats.

The Ambassador, Chris Stevens, and the three others who died were men of unusual courage who died heroically protecting their mission. The best tribute to the Ambassador comes from the mourning in the streets that we saw from the citizens of Benghazi and of Libya. It must be said that Ambassador Stevens did something that you rarely see in diplomatic work across the world. In little more than a few months after the Arab Spring, he had already established an entirely new and promising relationship between the United States of America and Libya. What an extraordinary man he must have been.

So I thank you, Mr. Chairman, for holding this hearing this afternoon, even in the midst of a campaign. It was and is important to hold a hearing now, when memories are fresh. And I certainly want to go on record for thanking the State Department, especially Ambassador Clinton, for what the chairman says has been the very open cooperation of the Department with this hearing.

I want to suggest that when there has been loss of life of this kind in service to the United States, there can be no difference between Democrats and Republicans in desiring a hearing to discover exactly what transpired. That is why I regret that the spirit of bipartisanship and openness that came from the State Department has not occurred here in this committee, that there has not been the sharing of information and witnesses so that both sides could be prepared to question witnesses and find out exactly what has happened.

I yield the remainder of my time to Mr. Connolly.

Mr. Connolly. I thank my colleague. And I welcome the witnesses here today. I join my colleagues in expressing the desire for a bipartisan inquiry. And I certainly hope that the committee will endeavor to make it genuinely bipartisan. I regret the fact that a trip to Libya occurred with no members of this side of the aisle in attendance. I had the privilege of going with David Dreier, the Republican chairman of the Rules Committee, to Libya in May. It is an inherently unstable situation. It was then, it is now. It is one we Americans hope will stabilize over time. I certainly hope that today's hearing is not going to be perceived as an effort to exploit a tragedy for political purposes 27 days out from an election. I hope in fact it is the down payment of a serious inquiry into how can we make this kind of thing not recur? How can we redouble our efforts to provide security to the brave men and women who serve in our Foreign Service? How can we make sure that we take a fresh look at the resources required and make sure, on a bipartisan basis, we are providing them?

So no good is done to the security of the United States to politicize this tragedy. And I can't imagine that the late Ambassador Chris Stevens would want us to do that. And so I hope that we will proceed in a bipartisan way and get to the bottom of not only what happened, but what are the forces at work that led to that. Far beyond just the issue of what our failures were, what is the nature of the challenge we face in countries like Libya post-Arab Spring?

Thank you, and I thank my colleague for yielding.

Chairman Issa. Thank you. I might note that the funding that is currently enjoyed by the State Department was voted bipartisan, one more Democrat voting for the appropriations than Republicans. So hopefully we now can understand how bipartisan it was. In fact, it was voted by more Democrats than Republicans.

The chair will now recognize our panel of witnesses. First of all, Lieutenant Colonel Andrew Wood is a member of the Utah National Guard and, I believe, a Department of Interior employee. Mr. Eric Nordstrom is a regional security officer at the United States Department of State. Ambassador Patrick J. Kennedy is Under Secretary for Management at the Department of State, and a frequent witness. Ms. Charlene Lamb is a Deputy Assistant Secretary for International Programs at the U.S. Department of State.

I want to welcome you. And pursuant to our rules, I would ask that you rise to take the oath. Raise your right hands. Do you solemnly swear or affirm that the testimony you are about to give will be the truth, the whole truth, and nothing but the truth?

Let the record reflect that all witnesses answered in the affirmative. Please take your seats.

Pursuant to our rules and tradition, each witness will have 5 minutes. Please, when you see your time expiring, wrap up. Your entire prepared statements will be placed in the record. I will take a moment only to admonish that Colonel Wood, we got yours fairly late, but we understand that this is not a regular shtick for you. For the administration, I am a little disappointed. We do have a 24-hour rule. And Ambassador Kennedy, if you would take back that it arrived, it is in, but we would appreciate in the future getting it a little earlier, because I think members on both sides pore over it.

With that, we recognize Lieutenant Colonel Wood.

WITNESS STATEMENTS

STATEMENT OF ANDREW WOOD

Colonel Wood. Thank you. I am Lieutenant Colonel Andrew Wood. I am a member of the Utah National Guard, with 24 years of service as a Special Forces soldier. I was mobilized for the Winter Olympics in 2002, Afghanistan from September of 2003 to May of 2004, and for counterterrorism work in the southern Philippines in August of 2007 to May of 2008. I currently work for the U.S. Bureau of Reclamation as an Upper Colorado regional security officer. I am responsible to Reclamation for a security program that oversees 58 high and significant hazard dams in five Western states, one of which is Glen Canyon Dam, a national critical infrastructure facility.

Upon hearing of the death of Ambassador Stevens, and later the congressional inquiry, I identified myself to my congressional representative's staff as a person with intimate knowledge of the security situation prior to the attack. I was subsequently contacted, and began a dialogue with staff investigators.

I made a personal decision to come forward with information, and do not represent DOD or any government agency. I had unique access and placement to many government leaders and agencies while working in Libya. I feel duty bound to come forward in order to inform and provide a portion of ground truth information. I feel a sense of honor for those individuals who have died in the service of their country. I realize much of my work in Libya was entangled in sensitive government work, and I must be careful not to betray the trust and confidences that have been placed in me. The killing of a U.S. Ambassador is a rare and extraordinary thing, and requires our attention as a people. As a citizen, I made the determination that this outweighs all other interests, and will risk whatever circumstances may result from my testimony.

I served as Site Security Team commander in Libya from 12 February to 14 August of this year, 2012. I was mobilized from the Utah National Guard in title 10 status and reported to Special Operations Command Africa, SOCAFRICA, which serves directly under AFRICOM. I was detailed in title 22 status to the Department of State and assumed command of the SST. The SST element consisted of 16 members. It is my understanding that it was drafted by the National Security Council to meet the demanding security challenges facing the Department of State and their requirement to reestablish diplomatic relations with a post-Qadhafi or free Libya. The SST loaned considerable support to the Department of State's security posture in this uncertain and volatile environment.

The SST's mission was to support and answer to the chief of mission in Libya. I worked directly for the regional security officer. We provided security support, medical support, communications support, for every facet of security that covered the embassy.

As the SST commander, I had a seat on the country team. I was closely involved with the operational planning and support to the RSO's security objectives. The embassy staff lived and worked together at two locations, in Tripoli and embassy property in Benghazi. The SST supported security movements for diplomatic officers in and around Tripoli and other parts of Libya as their work required. On two occasions I sent SST members to Benghazi to support and bolster security at that location. The SST was closely integrated with regular diplomatic security agents working directly for the RSO, as well as Mobile Security Deployment teams.

I traveled to Benghazi on two occasions with the RSO, once with the RSO to evaluate the security situation there, and once to conduct some work for the defense attache's office. I was there a second time in June when the U.K. ambassador's convoy was attacked. I responded with DS agents in order to help provide medical and security assistance to wounded U.K. security personnel. I conducted a post-attack investigation ofthe ambush or assault.

I regularly met with and held frequent conversations with Ambassadors Cretz and Stevens and other members of the security team. In June, when Eric Nordstrom rotated out, I was the senior member of the country team with the exception of Ambassador Stevens. We lived and worked closely together in an atmosphere that is common to an expeditionary post. Ambassador Stevens was an avid runner, and played tennis as well. The SST was heavily involved in performing his security detail when he ran. I ran with him on several occasions.

The SST provided an important link for the country team to SOCAFRICA with its intelligence assets and resources. There was a good exchange of information between SOCAFRICA and the RSO. There was a great working relationship between SST and diplomatic security agents and the MSD members of the embassy post throughout Libya.

I reported three times a week through a video teleconference to SOCAFRICA and sent daily situation reports. I had the communications capability to provide a direct link to SOCAFRICA 24/7. I no longer have access to email or documents that I worked with on a daily basis, as much of this was contained on AFRICOM servers and computers that I worked through. My recollection of dates is mostly from memory, and I will need to re-access that information in order to specify dates with greater certainty.

The State Department's decision not to extend SST's security work beyond the 5th of August terminated our security work in this capacity. The military members of my team were in the process of changing status from title 22 back to title 10 shortly before my departure.

The situation on the ground was continuously updated with reports that I sent to my military chain of command and CC'd the RSO on. The RSO sent information on security and threats in a similar manner up his chain of command.

While the sound of gunfire in and around Tripoli subsided from February to April, the situation remained unstable. Libyans struggled with a transitional government that hesitated to make decisions, and were forced to rely upon local and tribal militias with varying degrees of loyalty. In late spring, the police were allowed to return to work to help with traffic, but were limited to that only. Fighting between militias was common when I departed. Militias appeared to be disintegrating into organizations resembling freelance criminal operations. Targeted attacks against Westerners were on the increase. In June, the Ambassador received a threat on Facebook, with a public announcement that he liked to run around the embassy compound in Tripoli. When I arrived in February, there were three MSD teams on the ground. Ambassador Cretz was confronted with having to lose one of those teams, and requested an equal number of regular diplomatic security agents. The Ambassador struggled with renewing the SST beyond April 5th. That is Ambassador Stevens. The second MSD team was withdrawn shortly after Ambassador Cretz's departure, and the last MSD team was restricted to performing security work only--restricted from performing security work only, and limited only to training local guard force members in July. The remaining MSD was withdrawn at about the same time the SST security work was terminated. The RSO struggled to maintain these losses with regular diplomatic security personnel.

The security in Benghazi was a struggle, and remained a struggle throughout my time there. The situation remained uncertain, and reports from some Libyans indicated it was getting worse. Diplomatic security remained weak. In April, there was only one U.S. diplomatic security agent stationed there. The RSO struggled to obtain additional personnel, but there was never--but was never able to attain the numbers he felt comfortable with.

I hope the information I provide will be put together with data points from others so an accurate picture can be obtained. We need to be dedicated to the understanding--to understand the problems that surrounded this attack in order to find a solution. Our failure to do so will result in repeated instances that allow our adversaries to take an advantage over us. My purpose in conveying this information is to prevent their ability to take the life of another ambassador or kill another valuable and talented public servant working for the diplomatic service of their country.

Chairman Issa. Thank you.

Chairman Issa. Mr. Nordstrom.

STATEMENT OF ERIC ALLAN NORDSTROM

Mr. Nordstrom. Good morning, Chairman Issa, Ranking Member Cummings, and other distinguished members of the committee. My name is Eric Nordstrom, and I currently serve as a Supervisory Special Agent with the U.S. Department of State's Bureau of diplomatic security. I joined the Department in April 1998, and I have served in domestic and overseas postings, including Washington, D.C., Tegucigalpa, Honduras; Addis Ababa, Ethiopia; New Delhi, India; and most recently as the regional security officer at the U.S. embassy in Tripoli, Libya, a position I held from September 21st, 2011, until July 26th, 2012. As the regional security officer, or RSO, at the U.S. embassy in Tripoli, I served as the principal adviser to Ambassadors Cretz and Stevens on security and law enforcement matters.

I am here today to provide testimony in support of your inquiry into the tragic events of September 11, 2012, including the murders of Ambassador Stevens, Sean Smith, Glen Doherty, and Tyrone Woods. I had the pleasure of working with Ambassador Stevens during the final months of my tour in Libya, and would echo what many are saying, the loss of Ambassador Stevens is not only tragic for his family and sad for our country, but his death will prove to be a devastating loss for Libya, struggling to recover from its recent civil war. My family and I would like to offer our personal condolences to the families of these four patriots who gave their lives in the service of their country.

My contribution to our Nation's efforts in Libya will prove to be only a small part of a wider effort. There were many of us dedicated to the mission in Libya, both at home and abroad. To my colleagues who served with me and to those who are presently there in the aftermath of this attack, you have your country's sincere thanks and prayers.

Let me say a word about the evening of September 11th. I had not seen an attack of such ferocity and intensity previously in Libya, nor in my time with the diplomatic security Service. I am concerned that this attack signals a new security reality, just as the 1983 Beirut Marine barracks bombings did for the Marines, the 1998 East Africa embassy bombings did for the State Department, and 9/11 did for our entire country. However, we must remember that it is critical that we balance our risk mitigation efforts with the needs of our diplomats to do their jobs. The answer cannot be to operate from a bunker. Arriving in Tripoli in the midst of the Libyan civil war, it was immediately obvious to me that the post-revolution Libya was a weakened state, exhausted from their civil war, and operating under fragmented and paralyzed government institutions. They were barely able to protect themselves from armed gangs, Qadhafi loyalists, or roving militias. As a result, the Libyan temporary government was unable to extend security assets to diplomatic missions in customary ways that we expect around the world. We could not rely on the Libyan Government for security, intelligence, and law enforcement help to identify emerging threats or to ask them for assistance in mitigating those threats.

In Benghazi, however, the government of Libya, through the 17th February Martyrs Brigade, was able to provide us consistent armed security since the very earliest days of the revolution. Routine civil unrest, militia on militia violence, general lawlessness, and surprisingly, motor vehicle accidents, were the primary threats facing our mission and personnel during my time in Libya.

As Colonel Wood noted, in the spring of 2012 we noted an increasing number of attacks and incidents which appeared to target foreign-affiliated organizations. In response to these incidents, we implemented a number of changes to our security posture designed to mitigate those threats and disrupt any planning by would be attackers. Those efforts included reviewing and practicing our emergency preparedness drills, and most importantly, we reiterated our requests at all levels of government for a consistent armed host nation security force to support the mission. We also requested security staffing and extensions of the DOD Security Support Team. In my opinion, the primary security staffing issue that we dealt with was maintaining U.S. security personnel, whether diplomatic security agents or Security Support Team members, for a sufficient amount of time to enable the full training and deployment of a local bodyguard unit.

In early July 2012, prior to my departure, post requested continued TDY staffing of 15 U.S. security professionals, either DS field office agents, Mobile Security Deployment agents, or DOD/SST personnel, plus retention of a six-agent Mobile Security Deployment training team that would work with our newly created bodyguard unit. Earlier post extension requests for our DOD/SS Team in November 2011 and March 2012 were approved. Also, in March 2012 I requested DS staffing levels in Tripoli of five full-time agents to be permanently assigned there, 12 temporary duty DS agents, and six Mobile Security Deployment DS agents, again to train our newly created bodyguard unit. A request to maintain a level of five TDY DS agents in Benghazi was included in that same March 2012 request. Our long term security plan in Libya was to deploy an armed, locally hired Libyan bodyguard unit. Due to Libyan political sensitivities, armed private security companies were not allowed to operate in Libya. That was the case under Qadhafi, and that was the case under the free Libya.

Our existing uniformed static local guard force, both in Tripoli and Benghazi, were unarmed, similar to our local guard forces at many other posts around the world. Their job is simple. It is to observe, report, and alert armed host nation security or armed response forces, possibly DS agents if that's the case. The use of local nationals as armed bodyguards is a routine practice in the Department, and we often do so to comply with the local firearms regulations of the host nation.

Local nationals provide us with continuity, local expertise, threat awareness in their community, and language and cultural skills. I am confident that the committee will conclude that officers and employees of the Department of State diplomatic security service and mission Libya conducted themselves professionally, and with careful attention to managing the people and budgets in a way that reflected the gravity of the task.

I am proud of the work that our team accomplished in Libya under extraordinarily difficult circumstances. The protection of our Nation's diplomats, our embassies and consulates, and the work produced there is deserving of the time and treasure invested.

I am glad to further discuss my experiences, and hope it provides beneficial to the committee, the State Department and my fellow DS agents who are protecting and advancing U.S. interests abroad. Thank you, Mr. Chairman and members of the committee, for the opportunity to appear before you today. May God bless our country as we work towards peace in a contentious world. I stand ready to answer any questions that you might have of me.

Chairman Issa. Thank you.

Chairman Issa. Ms. Lamb?

STATEMENT OF CHARLENE R. LAMB

Ms. Lamb. Chairman Issa----

Chairman Issa. Could you turn your mic on, please?

Ms. Lamb. I am sorry.

Chairman Issa. That's all right. It is your first time.

Ms. Lamb. Chairman Issa, Ranking Member Cummings, members of the committee, my name is Charlene Lamb. I am Deputy Assistant Secretary for International Programs in the Bureau of diplomatic security at the Department of State. I have been in law enforcement for 35 years, including 17 consecutive years stationed abroad as a regional security officer in Nicaragua, Tanzania, Kuwait, Guatemala, and Germany. I am here today to share our best information to date about what happened in Benghazi on September 11th.

As you know, there are ongoing investigations and reviews being conducted, and we are speaking today with an incomplete picture. But as this process moves forward and more information becomes available, we will continue to engage closely with Congress.

Let me begin by describing the actual compound in Benghazi. It is more than 300 yards long and nearly 100 yards wide. The main building was divided into two sections. The public section included common areas and meeting space. The private section was a residential area that included a safe haven. A second building, Building B, housed diplomatic security agents. The tactical operations center occupied a third building. The fourth building on the compound served as barracks for the Libyan 17th February Brigade members.

After acquiring the compound, we made a number of security upgrades. Among other steps, we extended the height of the outer wall to 12 feet, with masonry concrete, barbed wire, and concertina razor wire. We increased the external lighting and erected Jersey barriers outside the perimeter. We also added equipment to detect explosives, as well as an imminent danger notification system. We installed security grills on windows accessible from the ground, and included escape windows with emergency releases.

There were five diplomatic security agents on the compound September 11th. There were also three members of the Libyan 17th February Brigade. In addition, a well trained U.S. quick reaction security team was stationed nearby at the embassy annex.

All of these measures and upgrades were taken in coordination with security officials in Benghazi, Tripoli, and Washington. I work closely with more than 275 facilities around the world, determining the right level of security for each one. It is an intensive, ongoing, constantly evolving process, one that I appreciate and understand from my own time on the ground as a diplomatic security officer.

That brings me to the events of September 11th itself. At approximately 9:40 p.m. local time, dozens of attackers launched a full scale assault. They forced their way through the pedestrian gate, used diesel fuel to set fire to the Libyan 17th February Brigade members' barracks, and then proceeded towards the main building. A diplomatic security agent working in the Tactical Operations Center immediately activated the imminent danger notification system. He also alerted the quick reaction security team stationed nearby, the Libyan 17th February Brigade, the embassy in Tripoli, and the diplomatic security Command Center in Washington.

One agent secured Ambassador Stevens and Sean Smith, the information management officer, in a safe haven. The attackers used diesel fuel to set the main building ablaze. Thick smoke rapidly filled the entire structure. The agent began leading the Ambassador and Sean Smith toward the emergency escape window. Nearing unconsciousness himself, the agent opened the emergency escape grill window and crawled out. He then realized they had become separated in the smoke, so he reentered and searched the building multiple times. Finally, the agent, suffering from severe smoke inhalation, barely able to breathe or speak, exited to the roof. Other agents retrieved their M4 submachine guns from Building B. When they attempted to return to the main building, they encountered armed attackers and doubled back. They regrouped, made their way to a nearby armored vehicle, and then drove over to assist the agent on the roof in search for the Ambassador and Mr. Smith. After numerous attempts, they found Mr. Smith. Unfortunately, he was already deceased. They still could not find the Ambassador.

The quick reaction security team arrived with 40 members of the Libyan 17th February Brigade. They all continued the search for the Ambassador. Then, at approximately 11 p.m., the Libyans insisted for everyone's safety they needed to evacuate the site. The combined security team made a final search for the Ambassador before leaving the annex in an armored vehicle.

Ms. Lamb. They took heavy fire as they pulled away from the main building and on the street outside the compound but were able to make their way to the annex----

Mr. Chaffetz. Point of order. Point of order.

Chairman Issa. The gentlelady will suspend.

The gentleman will state his point of order.

Mr. Chaffetz. Mr. Chairman, I am concerned that we are getting into classified issues that deal with sources and methods that would be totally inappropriate in an open forum such as this.

Chairman Issa. The gentlelady, Ms. Lamb, Mr. Kennedy, is it your intent to declassify any or all material in Ms. Lamb's statement?

Mr. Kennedy. Mr. Chairman, Mr. Chaffetz, the information that we are presenting today in open session is entirely unclassified.

Mr. Chaffetz. Mr. Chairman, I totally object to the use of that photo.

Chairman Issa. The gentleman will state his reason.

Mr. Chaffetz. I believe it to be classified information that goes to sources and methods and should not be disseminated in a public manner such as State is doing here today.

Mr. Cummings. Mr. Chairman?

Chairman Issa. Ranking Member?

Mr. Cummings. I was just wondering, these are people from the State Department. They apparently have clearance to show this information. I assume they wouldn't come here unless it was cleared. So I would just----

Chairman Issa. Yeah. I appreciate the gentleman's comments.

Ambassador, it is your statement that these either are now declassified or you are declassifying them at this hearing; is that correct? In other words, is this cleared through your channels to be given here today?

Mr. Kennedy. This information is available, sir, for public dissemination, yes, sir.

Chairman Issa. Okay.

Colonel Wood. You can Google this.

Chairman Issa. The gentleman's point of order, although noted--it is the prerogative of the executive branch to determine what is not classified.

The one thing I would note, my able staff has compared last night's press conference and the opening statement of Ms. Lamb, and it appears as though her opening statement should have been given to us last night since it was obviously the one given to the press.

We will reset----

Mr. Chaffetz. Mr. Chairman?

Chairman Issa. Yes? The gentleman will state his comment.

Mr. Chaffetz. Can I make one more comment?

I was told specifically while I was in Libya I could not and should not ever talk about what you are showing here today.

Mr. Kennedy. Mr. Chairman, if I might, this is commercial digital imagery that we--from a commercial satellite source, sir.

Chairman Issa. Well, I appreciate that. Ultimately, I am going to side with the administration, that you have a right to show what you want to show and consider it unclassified.

I would, again, recognize that we were shown documents this morning in camera that said unclassified, but they weren't turned over to the committee. If you have anything else that you intend to use, if it hasn't been provided to the committee, I would strongly suggest that that binder and other materials be provided at this time.

Again, it is your prerogative to declassify. It is not your prerogative to selectively tell a Member of Congress something is classified and then come to an open hearing and say it is not. Since Mr. Chaffetz visited with your people, people that work for you, Mr. Kennedy, Secretary Kennedy, I would ask that you rectify this in the future.

The gentlelady may----

Mr. Cummings. Mr. Chairman?

Chairman Issa. I have ruled that they----

Mr. Cummings. I just have a question, a point of order, Mr. Chairman. I just have one question so that we will be clear, because we don't want any misconceptions.

Just, Ambassador, can we get that on Google?

Chairman Issa. This is not a point of order.

Mr. Cummings. I just--I want to know. I mean, I am just curious.

Chairman Issa. The ranking member----

Mr. Cummings. Thank you for letting me ask my question.

Chairman Issa. --is not stating a point of order.

Mr. Cummings. Thank you.

Chairman Issa. Thank you.

Please reset it for 2 minutes.

If you could finish within 2 minutes, Ms. Lamb, we would appreciate it.

Ms. Lamb. Yes.

Chairman Issa. The gentlelady is recognized.

Ms. Lamb. Thank you.

In the early morning, an additional security team arrived from Tripoli and proceeded to the annex. Shortly after they arrived, the annex started taking mortar fire, with as many as three direct hits on the compound. It was during this mortar attack that Tyrone Woods and Glen Doherty were killed and a diplomatic security agent and a quick reaction security team were critically wounded.

A large number of Libyan Government security officers subsequently arrived and escorted the remaining Americans to the airport. We were then able to confirm reports that the Ambassador's body was at the Benghazi General Hospital, and the Department coordinated the transfer of his remains to the airport.

Before I close, I would like to say: The men and women who risked their lives in the service of our country are heroes. I have served with many of our security professionals around the world. They are my friends and my colleagues, and I trust them with my life.

Thank you.

Chairman Issa. Thank you.

Chairman Issa. I would direct that that chart be taken down.

Upon further reflection, you know, although commercially available, in this hearing room we are not going to point out details of what may still, in fact, be a facility of the United States Government or more facilities.

So you may continue. I respect your right to deliver what you want. But I will caution, once again, Ambassador, that that which is told to us on a classified basis needs to remain that way. You can't have it one day a classified briefing, which I attended yesterday, and then the same--substantially same material be presented unclassified the next day.

The Ambassador is recognized.

STATEMENT OF THE HON. PATRICK F. KENNEDY

Mr. Kennedy. Thank you very much.

Chairman Issa, Ranking Member Cummings, distinguished members of the committee, I would like to share a few words with you. Quote, ``Libyans face significant challenges as they make the transition from an oppressive dictatorship to a stable and prosperous democracy, but it is clearly in the U.S. interest and it will be an extraordinary honor to represent the United States during this historic period of transition in Libya.''

Those were Ambassador Stevens's words at his confirmation hearing, and they help us understand why he went to Libya, his passion for the country, its people, and the mission. He believed that no challenge was too big or too hard if our national security interest and our values were at stake. And that is what is at stake in Libya.

At your request, in the spirit of cooperation, we are here today to do our best to answer your questions. But I ask you to understand that we do not yet know all the answers or results of ongoing reviews. And there may be, as the chairman had noted, information that is classified and can only be dealt with in classified session.

As Secretary Clinton has said, the American people, especially the families who lost loved ones, deserve a full and accurate accounting. We at the State Department are determined to get this right, and nobody will hold us more accountable than we hold ourselves. We lost friends and colleagues, a cross-section of those who put their lives on the line every day in the inherently dangerous work of diplomatic service to our Nation.

The Secretary has already appointed an accountability review board and has begun working to determine whether our security systems and procedures were appropriate in light of the threat environment, whether they were properly implemented, as well as any lessons that may impact our work around the world. The Secretary has asked us to work as quickly and transparently as possible without sacrificing diligence and accuracy.

This is a complicated review that will take time as we learn more about what happened and as we are better able to assess the information we have. Until then, it is an incomplete picture, and, as a result, our answers today will also be incomplete.

No one in the administration has claimed to know for certain all the answers. We have always made clear that we are giving the best information we have at the time, and that information has evolved. For example, if any administration official, including any career official, were on television on Sunday, September 16th, they would have said what Ambassador Rice said. The information she had at that point from the intelligence community is the same that I had at that point. Clearly, we know more today than what we did on the Sunday, September 17th, after the attack. But we will continue consulting with you throughout this process.

I would like to address a broader question that may be on your minds: Why is the United States in Benghazi when there are real dangers there? This question does go to the heart of what we do for the State Department and America's role in the world.

Ambassador Stevens arrived in Benghazi during the height of the revolution. The city was at the heart of the opposition to Colonel Qadhafi, and the rebels there were fighting for their lives. It was dangerous. A bomb exploded in the parking lot of his hotel. The transitional authorities struggled to provide basic security. Extremists thought to exploit their own agenda.

But Chris understood that the State Department must operate in places where our military cannot or does not, there are no other boots on the ground, and where there are serious threats to our security. He understood that the new Libya was being born in Benghazi and it was critical that we have an active presence there.

That is why Ambassador Stevens stayed in Benghazi in those difficult days and returned as Ambassador as the Libyans began their difficult transition to democracy. He knew his mission was vital to our interests and values and was an investment that would pay off in a strong partnership with a free Libya.

After the September 11 attack, the Libyan people showed how right he was. Thousands marched in the streets of Benghazi, mourning their fallen friend with signs saying, ``Chris Stevens was a friend to all Libyans.'' They overran extremist bases. Civilians insisted that the militia disarm and support the new democracy. They confirmed what Chris Stevens knew so well: The United States is better off because he went to Benghazi.

We must review the security procedures in place and improve them, asking ourselves if our people had what they needed and how we can reduce the risk of this happening again. But one thing is not up for debate today or any other day: Those who risk their lives in the service of our country are heroes, and we must support them, particularly those who provide security in an unsecure environment.

Diplomacy must be practiced in dangerous places. The United States sends people to more than 275 diplomatic posts. No other agency is asked to stretch so far. We do this because we have learned that when America is absent, especially from dangerous places, there are consequences. Extremism takes root, our interests suffer, and our security is threatened.

As the Secretary says, leadership means showing up. That is what we do. That is how we protect this country and sustain its global leadership. We can and we will reduce the risk to those who serve, but no one can eliminate it. Our facilities must be protected, but not all are fortresses.

I want to be clear: We regularly assess risk and resource allocation, a process involving the considered judgments of experienced professionals on the ground and in Washington using the best available information. The assault that occurred on the evening of September 17th, however, was an unprecedented assault by dozens of heavily armed men.

We must continue deploying our diplomats and development professionals to dangerous places like Benghazi. There is no alternative. As the Secretary has said, we will not retreat, we will keep leading, and we will stay engaged everywhere in the world. All of us in the State Department will honor our fallen colleagues by continuing their work with the same purpose and resolve they demonstrated.

Mr. Chairman, thank you again for this opportunity. The Congress is a crucial partner in providing diplomatic security, so I look forward to working with you and the members of this committee to continue providing America's diplomats with the support and resources needed to carry out their important work.

Thank you, sir.

Chairman Issa. Thank you.

Chairman Issa. Ambassador Kennedy, yesterday you made a significant press announcement. I want to ask you a couple of questions.

This morning, and only this morning, we were shown, our staff was shown a book, a binder in camera. The documents in that book all indicate unclassified. Are you prepared to deliver those documents to us at this time?

Mr. Kennedy. Mr. Chairman, my understanding is that we did make information available to the committee both last night and this morning, and we have that material still here. We would be glad to meet with the committee or committee staff afterwards.

Chairman Issa. No, we want it for this hearing. The information when looked at in camera was unclassified but, in fact, perhaps embarrassing. Will you make that information available at this time so I can circulate it to all the Members on the dais?

Mr. Kennedy. Mr. Chairman, the information--while individual pieces may be unclassified, the totality of the information is such that it must be considered to be restricted, and the context is all important.

Chairman Issa. I agree with you.

And, with that, I now move that the unclassified document of September 11th, 2012, appearing above the signature of the Ambassador, be placed in the record.

Without objection, so ordered.

And the staff will distribute it.

Additionally, I move that the document of March 28th, 2012, be placed in the record.

Without objection, so ordered.

Additionally--and these will have to be printed--the document of August 2nd, 2012, from the Ambassador, and of July 9th, 2012, be placed in the record.

Without objection, so ordered.

Mr. Cummings. Mr. Chairman?

Chairman Issa. Yes?

Mr. Cummings. Just so that we will be clear, you already have the documents? I just want to be clear, that is all.

Chairman Issa. In real time, a whistleblower has provided us with some of these documents. We confirmed that these documents are similar to the documents being--or, identical to the documents being withheld. It is the determination of the chair that these documents were responsive, unclassified, and appropriate for discovery.

Mr. Cummings. Mr. Chairman, I was just asking if you already had the documents.

Chairman Issa. Well, if you will notice, I am looking at one on an iPad.

Mr. Cummings. Yeah. You already have them. Okay, that is all I asked.

Chairman Issa. We do have them, and others. So they will be circulated.

Mr. Cummings. To both sides?

Chairman Issa. To both sides, of course.

Mr. Cummings. Thank you.

Chairman Issa. They are now documents of this hearing and of this--and before I do my opening statement, or before I do my questioning, Ambassador, I don't like doing this, but, ultimately, the cooperation we received has caused individuals to say things which are consistent with these documents which are being withheld. And since the documents are unclassified, we can reach no other conclusion but that they are inappropriate.

And, quite frankly, after my years in the military and my years on the Hill and my years on the Select Intelligence Committee, to say that a broad array of unclassified documents somehow in totality makes classified is to make everything you do unavailable to the Congress.

With that, we will begin the clock.

Mr. Nordstrom, you have done a lot of things that I appreciate in communication. October 1st, you sent a statement, an email to Mr.

Chaffetz. He read it in his opening statement. Do you stand by that statement?

Mr. Nordstrom. I do. That was a response, again, as a follow-up to our meeting on the same day where we discussed a number of documents that you were interested in getting, specifically the list of incidents that we had discussed.

Chairman Issa. In that statement, basically what you were saying is there wasn't sufficient resources provided, considering the escalating, the coming together of what could have and turned out to be a catastrophic attack. Would that be a fair paraphrasing of what you said?

Mr. Nordstrom. That was one of the main reasons I continued to ask for those resources, yes.

Chairman Issa. Now, we had an informal meeting with you, bipartisan meeting. In that, you relayed something I think is very important. I asked you about Ambassador Stevens, a very skilled career diplomat, and how he dealt with threats related to security. And you told me--I am paraphrasing--that, for example, when there was a perceived threat in his running, he ceased running.

Then, when both you and Colonel Wood were able to come up with an acceptable way that he could continue, by varying where he went and so on, he ran again, but only ran again under your authority and your recommendation.

Is that correct?

Mr. Nordstrom. That is correct, Chairman.

Chairman Issa. And I think I asked you, was he a compliant officer? Did he do what you thought when you recommended it, or did he chafe at any time over what you thought was best for his security?

Mr. Nordstrom. At no time did I have any concerns raised to me by Ambassador Stevens.

Colonel Wood and I, senior member of the Mobile Security Deployment team, routinely met with him and discussed general threats but also specific concerns that we might have about his schedule, his routine, and his meetings.

As I noted, in that informal hearing, you know, one of the specific threats that we had received that was referenced this morning was a threat that was posted to Facebook. We came across that threat as a result of Senator McCain coming out to post to review the elections that were held in early July. There had been some postings about that.

But my point of is that he was absolutely responsive, and he deferred to what our concerns were.

Chairman Issa. Thank you.

Ms. Lamb, yesterday you told us in testimony that you received from Mr. Nordstrom a recommendation but not a request for more security. And you admitted that, in fact, you had previously said that if he submitted a request, you would not support it. Is that correct?

Ms. Lamb. Sir, after our meeting last night, I went back and--at the time----

Chairman Issa. Well, first answer the question, then I will let you expand. Did you say that yesterday, that you would not support it if he gave you the request?

Ms. Lamb. Under the current conditions, yes.

Chairman Issa. Okay. And then last night you discovered what?

Ms. Lamb. I went back and reviewed the July 9 cable from which I was referring, and that was not in that cable. I have been reviewing lots of documents----

Chairman Issa. Well, we have a July 9th cable--it is one of them that I put in the record----

Ms. Lamb. Yes.

Chairman Issa. --that, in fact, has the word ``request.'' It doesn't meet your standard of, perhaps, what you call a formal request; you described that. But it does request more assets.

If you looked at the July 9th, 2012, cable--and this is less than 60 days, or roughly 60 days beforehand--it says, ``Summary and action request. Embassy Tripoli requests continued TDY security support for an additional 60 days.''

Now, yesterday you told us, under penalty of perjury, essentially, that it wasn't a request, it was a recommendation. Does the word ``request'' mean ``request''? And are you prepared to say today that they requested these assets above and beyond what they had on September 11th, rather than that they simply recommended?

Ms. Lamb. Sir, we discussed that there was no justification that normally comes with a request. That cable was a very detailed and complex cable outlining what----

Chairman Issa. Right. Well, we have now read that cable, and you are right, it is detailed. And in several more places it expresses concerns.

The September 11th cable from the now-deceased Ambassador expresses current concerns on that day. Repeatedly in the cables that were denied to us what we see is people telling you that al-Qaeda-type organizations are coming together.

Now, the problem I have is that the State Department is basically saying, Mr. Nordstrom didn't do his job; he didn't make a formal request with justification. The Ambassador didn't do his job; he didn't make a good enough case. And that is what you are standing behind here today, in addition to saying, well, there were five people there, therefore.

An embassy--a compound owned by us and serving like a consulate was, in fact, breached less than 60 days before, approximately 60 days before the murder of the Ambassador in that facility. Isn't that true?

Ms. Lamb. Sir, we had the correct number of assets in Benghazi at the time of 9/11 for what had been agreed upon.

Chairman Issa. Okay, my time has expired. To start off by saying you had the correct number, and our Ambassador and three other individuals are dead and people are in the hospital recovering because it only took moments to breach that facility, somehow doesn't seem to ring true to the American people.

With that, I recognize the ranking member.

Mr. Cummings, have you received the copies of the cables yet?

Mr. Cummings. Yeah. Thank you.

Chairman Issa. Okay.

Mr. Cummings. Thank you.

Mr. Nordstrom, you testified here today--your testimony here today paints a different picture than what has been portrayed in the press. In your testimony, you stated that you were, quote, ``impressed with the plans that would send our team into Libya, a massive show of well-organized resources,'' end of quote.

You further explained that, and I quote, ``The Department of State Diplomatic Security Service, and Mission Libya officers conducted themselves professionally and with careful attention to managing people and budgets in a way that reflects the gravity of that task.''

Did you say that?

Mr. Nordstrom. Yes, I did, sir.

Mr. Cummings. And you stated that you felt that the vast majority of your resource requests were, and I quote, ``considered seriously and fastidiously by DS and the Department,'' end of quote. Did you say that?

Mr. Nordstrom. Absolutely.

Mr. Cummings. Did you mean that?

Mr. Nordstrom. Absolutely.

Mr. Cummings. In fact, you list out a litany of security improvements that you were able to make in both Benghazi and Tripoli.

I think all of that is helpful to put into context the concerns that you have raised about staffing numbers.

In your interview on October 1st, 2012, you told the committee that you thought that there should be five diplomatic security special agents stationed in Benghazi and that you sent two cables, one in March and one in July, making that request. Is that right?

Mr. Nordstrom. That is correct. And if I could add to that point, it was not my decision to come up with the five agents in Benghazi. That number originated from a December 2011 cable detailing the future of operations in Benghazi.

Mr. Cummings. All right.

Mr. Nordstrom. That cable was drafted in the Department. I had at no time an opportunity to add or comment on that. However, the principal officer in Benghazi had an opportunity to comment on that. It was that number, five, which DS had committed to which we continued to ask them to meet throughout my time there.

Mr. Cummings. Now, we have reviewed that July cable, and it states further, ``Post anticipates''--and I quote, ``Post anticipates supporting operations in Benghazi with at least one permanently assigned RSO from Tripoli; however, would request continued TDY support to fill a minimum of three security positions in Benghazi.''

So that would be a total of four; is that right?

Mr. Nordstrom. That is correct.

Mr. Cummings. I understand that you left Libya before the attacks; is that right?

Mr. Nordstrom. That is absolutely correct.

Mr. Cummings. Ambassador Kennedy, let me turn to you. We have now been told there were, in fact, five--five--special agents in Benghazi the night of the attack, contrary to press reports.

Can you verify whether, in fact, there were five special agents in Benghazi on the night of the attack? Were there also any additional armed guards at the compound on that night?

Could you answer those two questions, please?

Mr. Kennedy. Yes, sir. There were five diplomatic security special agents on the compound the evening of September 11th. And there were three additional armed security personnel provided by the Government of Libya.

Mr. Cummings. Now, Agent Lamb, how do you respond to concerns that you failed to respond to requests for additional special agents in Benghazi? You know, that is a serious charge there.

Ms. Lamb. Yes, sir. And we have evaluated that; I have evaluated it both with Eric Nordstrom and with a senior RSO that spent TDY time there, as well. I asked them to do a serious assessment of the numbers that were needed there.

When Mr. Nordstrom and I discussed the duties of the agents out in Benghazi, they were using one agent to drive the vehicle, and they were using another agent to watch classified communications equipment 24/7. So these are not normally duties that are assigned to DS agents.

So I just--I asked Eric to review that. And when Renee Crowningshield, another RSO, went to Benghazi, was also asked to review the numbers.

And Eric worked closely with post management, asked them to hire a driver, and we hired a driver, trained a driver. And then the driver took the place of what the DS agent was doing. And then they came up, through technical security means, a way around the need to have the 24/7 coverage.

Mr. Cummings. One last question: When the Ambassador traveled to Benghazi before the attack, could the security team in Tripoli have sent additional agents with him if they thought it was necessary?

Ms. Lamb. Absolutely.

Mr. Cummings. Very well.

Chairman Issa. Would the gentleman yield?

Mr. Cummings. Yes.

Chairman Issa. Were any of those five DS agents that were there from Tripoli that had come down with the Ambassador?

Ms. Lamb. Two had traveled with the Ambassador.

Chairman Issa. Okay. So, for the record, there were three there and two happened to be there because the Ambassador was there. That is not the same as five being in Benghazi ordinarily.

Ms. Lamb. No, sir.

Chairman Issa. So if in the ordinary course there had been five, there still would have been two more coming down with the Ambassador, for a total of seven.

Ms. Lamb. But post had agreed that three was a sufficient number to have on the ground.

Mr. Cummings. So, just one question.

Chairman Issa. Of course.

Mr. Cummings. So, Mr. Nordstrom, the cable we talked about asked for four agents, not five; is that right?

Mr. Nordstrom. If you could just clarify which cable? As I said, I sent a number of requests back by cable.

Mr. Cummings. The July cable.

Mr. Nordstrom. July 9th?

Mr. Cummings. Yes. It asked for four and not five.

Mr. Nordstrom. It asked for a minimum of three. And our plan was--at the time, we had three full-time permanently assigned agents in Libya: myself and two assistants.

Mr. Cummings. So, even so, there were five on the night of the attack; is that right?

Mr. Nordstrom. That is my understanding, although I was not there.

Mr. Cummings. All right, thank you.

Chairman Issa. I thank the gentleman.

We now recognize the former chairman of the full committee for his questions, Mr. Burton.

Mr. Burton. Thank you, Mr. Chairman.

Mr. Kennedy, right after the September 11th attack, you were up here on Capitol Hill giving a briefing to aides, and you indicated--in fact, you said that this appeared to be a terrorist attack. Do you stand by that?

Mr. Kennedy. What I said, Mr. Chairman, is that I was--former chairman, Mr. Burton, sir----

Chairman Issa. Once a chairman, always a chairman.

Mr. Burton. Yeah, right.

Mr. Kennedy. The question I recall being asked was, was this a premeditated attack. And I responded----

Mr. Burton. It says----

Mr. Kennedy. I responded to that that I am not prepared to render a formal opinion on whether or not it was premeditated, but I thought it involved a degree of complexity that was significant.

Mr. Burton. Well, according to people who were there, you called it a terrorist attack.

Mr. Kennedy. Oh. That was--in a separate statement, yes, sir, I said----

Mr. Burton. Okay. That is all I wanted to know.

Mr. Kennedy. Yes, sir.

Mr. Burton. That is all I wanted to know.

Mr. Kennedy. Absolutely.

Mr. Burton. Okay. Because today, as I listen to people--and you, Ms. Lamb, have said--you have described these attackers in a number of ways, but you don't mention terrorists at all. Why is that?

I mean, the compound had been attacked once before and breached. And these people had all these weapons--projectiles, grenades, all kinds of weapons. Why would you call this anything but a terrorist attack? And why do you call them attackers?

Ms. Lamb. Sir, I have just presented the facts as they have come across. I am not making any judgments on my own, and I am leaving that----

Mr. Burton. Okay, well, let me ask you a couple of other questions. There were 16 troops that were there at that compound, and they requested them to be kept there. And they sent a suggestion to you that they be kept there, and then you responded, saying that if that was presented to you, you would not accept that. Was that your sole decision?

Ms. Lamb. Sir, they were not in Benghazi. They were in Tripoli. I just want to make sure that we are----

Mr. Burton. I understand. Go ahead.

Ms. Lamb. Okay. And when the cable came in where RSO Nordstrom laid out all of his staffing requirements and needs, I asked our desk officer to go back and sit down with him, or through emails and telephone conversations, to work out all the details and line up exactly how many security personnel, armed security personnel, did he need.

Mr. Burton. Okay. Well----

Ms. Lamb. But----

Mr. Burton. You did not agree with that assessment that they needed those there.

Ms. Lamb. No, sir. We had been training----

Mr. Burton. No, no. I just want to know----

Ms. Lamb. --people, local Libyans----

Mr. Burton. --did you or did you not say that if that was presented to you, you would not accept it?

Ms. Lamb. He was post----

Mr. Burton. Did you or did you not say----

Ms. Lamb. Yes, sir. I said that, personally, I would not support it.

Mr. Burton. Okay. Now, why----

Ms. Lamb. He could request it.

Mr. Burton. --is that? Why is that?

Ms. Lamb. Because----

Mr. Burton. You knew about all these other attacks that had taken place. There had been 12, 14.

Ms. Lamb. We had been training local Libyans and arming them----

Mr. Burton. Well, now----

Ms. Lamb. --for almost a year.

Mr. Burton. Okay. Well, let me just interrupt and say that the local Libyan militia that was there, many of them supposedly were told by friends and relatives that there was going to be an imminent attack on that compound, and so many of them were left.

Ms. Lamb. Yes.

Mr. Burton. They didn't want to be involved in the attack.

Ms. Lamb. Sir, with----

Mr. Burton. Did--well, wait, wait, wait, wait.

Ms. Lamb. Okay.

Mr. Burton. Yeah.

Ms. Lamb. Sorry.

Mr. Burton. So I don't understand why you would say out of hand that you don't think those 16 troops should be there.

Ms. Lamb. Sir, with due respect, they were in Tripoli; they were not in Benghazi. And it would not have made any difference in Benghazi.

Mr. Burton. Okay.

Mr. Nordstrom, do you care to comment on this?

Mr. Nordstrom. As DAS Lamb indicated, beginning in about the January-February time frame, I had a number of conversations with DAS Lamb, with the regional director for Near Eastern Affairs, and also the desk officer for Libya itself. And a lot of those discussions were specific to determining what exactly our personnel needs were, looking at metrics, looking at what the duties would be that these personnel would be doing, be it DOD-sourced or Department of State-sourced.

The number that we continued to come up with--and it is generally the same number that was requested in March, in my first request-- was approximately 12 armed security, with an additional 6 persons that would be focused on training that local guard unit.

Chairman Issa. Would the gentleman yield?

Mr. Burton. I would be happy to yield.

Chairman Issa. Isn't it true--we had this in testimony by the other RSO yesterday from Benghazi--that they would have as much as 30 percent turnover per month in these people they were training; that, in fact, you were not getting, if you will, good career people to come in, but, in fact, had very high turnover both in the unarmed and, to a lesser extent, in the armed portion of the training.

Mr. Nordstrom. We had--just in terms of a point of clarification, we did have--the guard force was somewhat confusing. In Tripoli, the guards that we employed were directly hired by the Embassy. They were----

Chairman Issa. I am only speaking of Benghazi.

Mr. Nordstrom. Okay. Those were subcontracted. The decision to go with a contractor, Blue Mountain, was largely based on our concern of how long we would be in Benghazi. We were concerned that if we retained or brought on board full-time employees, we would have to then find a position for them if that post ever went away.

So, yes, it is my understanding that there was a very high turnover with those people.

In terms of the armed security that were there, the 17 February, it was a core group that stayed there largely for the duration.

Chairman Issa. The gentleman's time has expired, but, Colonel Wood, if you want to finish up on anything that is responsive, that would be fine.

Colonel Wood. Yes. The 16 members of the SST did go to Benghazi on two separate occasions to support movement of the principal officer in that location, to bolster the security that was there. She made trips to Tobruk and Derna, and they were needed there for the extra--just the extra movement that she had and to remain--to guard the compound and to provide a quick reaction force, if necessary.

We did that on, like I said, two separate occasions to provide that extra support. The SST on loan to the security force goes above and beyond normal, I guess, law enforcement-oriented security. These individuals were familiar with and carried larger-caliber, better weapons, and the tactics they would employ would be to counter a military-style attack.

Chairman Issa. Thank you.

Ms. Norton?

Ms. Norton. Thank you, Mr. Chairman.

Ambassador Kennedy, I want to make sure I clarify one of the most controversial parts of this matter, and that is how the public first learned of the first reason given for the disturbances in Benghazi.

Now, I understand that the State Department did not take any position, including the position taken by Ambassador Rice. So I think it is important to trace how the Ambassador came to the conclusions that she reported on television.

She said that her information was that the Benghazi matters were similar to the protests that had arisen in Cairo. And she referred to extremist elements, opportunistic elements taking advantage, essentially, of that protest.

Now, the Office of the Director of National Intelligence issued a statement that indicated that it had been the source of the Ambassador's statement. And I would like to read what the National Intelligence Director said.

``In the immediate aftermath, there was information that led us to assess that the attack began spontaneously, following protests earlier that day at our Embassy in Cairo. We provided that initial assessment to executive branch officials and Members of Congress, who used that information to discuss the attack publicly and to provide updates as they became available. Throughout our investigation, we continued to emphasize that information gathered was preliminary and evolving."

I note, by the way, that, Mr. Nordstrom, you say in your testimony--I am looking at page 2--that the ferocity and intensity of the attack was nothing that we had seen in Libya or that I had seen in my time--my entire time in diplomatic service, indicating that this was something of a surprise attack and, I might say, suggesting that perhaps we should be about rethinking how to protect our outposts, since it is clear we are not going to do it with lots of funds.

But what I read as the statement, Ambassador Kennedy, could I ask you, from the National Intelligence Director, could I ask you if you have any reason to doubt that Ambassador Rice relied on that information from the National Intelligence Director?

Mr. Kennedy. No, Ms. Norton. When I came up to give a briefing earlier that week, followed I think a day or 2 later by Ambassador Rice, both of us were relying on the same information. As I said in my oral statement, that if I or any other senior administration official, career or noncareer, would have been on that television show, other than Susan Rice, we would have said the same thing because we were drawing on the intelligence information that was then available to us.

This has been, as you all know, very much an evolving situation. What we knew that first week and that first weekend has evolved over time, so we know much more now than we knew then.

Ms. Norton. Indeed, the National Director issued a statement on the 28th, and he said, ``As we learned more about the attack, we revised our initial assessment to reflect new information indicating that it was a deliberate and organized terrorist attack carried out by extremists.'' So we see the evolving nature of it.

Look, I have to ask you about the diplomats who were stationed in Cairo who were accused by Governor Mitt Romney of sympathizing with the attackers. I would like to know how these diplomats, these personnel in Cairo reacted to that criticism.

Mr. Kennedy. I am afraid, Ms. Norton, I don't know. I have not had any conversations with the public affairs section in the Embassy in Cairo.

But I can assure you, from just my general knowledge of for 39 years in the foreign service, that there is not a foreign service officer or foreign service professional in our service who at all sympathizes or agrees with terrorists.

Chairman Issa. Thank you.

We now go to the gentleman from Ohio, Mr. Jordan.

Mr. Jordan. Thank you.

Chairman Issa. Could you yield me 10 seconds for a quick question?

Mr. Jordan. Sure.

Chairman Issa. Let's understand. What you are saying here today is that one piece of intel, one piece of intel got you guys, yourself and Ambassador Rice, to make a wrong statement 5 or 6 days later and still be making it? Because Sunday is a long time after Tuesday.

So you are saying that you got it wrong and it stayed wrong, you didn't know any better, between the 11th and the 16th; is that right?

Mr. Kennedy. The information that was available----

Chairman Issa. No, no, I just----

Mr. Kennedy. The information that was available from the intelligence community to both myself----

Chairman Issa. Ambassador----

Mr. Kennedy. --when I----

Chairman Issa. Ambassador--Ambassador, you are a great witness historically. I asked you, did you have any contrary knowledge over those 5 days? That is all I want.

Mr. Kennedy. No, sir.

Chairman Issa. Okay. You didn't know any better for the next 5 days is your testimony.

Thank you, Mr. Jordan.

Mr. Chaffetz. Mr. Chairman? May I ask unanimous consent that we give equal time to Mr. Cummings to respond and then give Mr. Jordan his full 5 minutes?

Mr. Lynch. Mr. Chairman, on that request----

Chairman Issa. To be honest--Mr. Lynch, are you requesting time?

Mr. Lynch. On a point of order. On a point of order.

Mr. Cummings. I was just----

Chairman Issa. I ask unanimous consent that the ranking member have 15 seconds.

Without objection, so ordered.

Mr. Lynch. On a point of order. Objection. Mr. Chairman, with all due respect, you just went over----

Chairman Issa. You don't have to apologize to me.

Mr. Lynch. With all due respect, you just allowed Mr. Burton to go over by 2 minutes, and you are giving Mr. Cummings 15 seconds. You know what I mean? There is a little bit----

Mr. Chaffetz. Mr. Chairman?

Mr. Lynch. I am sure you are going to balance out the time.

Chairman Issa. No, I understand. And we have gone over, both on witnesses and that. And I am going to pull it back into 5 minutes----

Mr. Lynch. There you go.

Chairman Issa. --very solidly.

Mr. Lynch. Okay. But just be fair to the ranking member.

Chairman Issa. Before we get down to your part of the dais, I will get there, I promise.

Mr. Lynch. Thank you, sir.

Mr. Chaffetz. Mr. Chairman, can I----

Chairman Issa. Thank you.

Without objection, the ranking member is given equal time to ask a question.

Please.

Mr. Cummings. Yeah, I just want to go back to you, Ambassador. I think Ms. Norton and the chairman asked a very critical question.

The chairman talked about the 5 days. Can you give us--can you try to explain that to us, that, you know, during that period of 5 days or whatever it was, not being able to--not having the information, contrary to what Ms. Rice may have said? And I understand that was based on intelligence, but can you explain how that could happen to the public?

In other words, were you all still gathering information? Was the State Department in the process of trying to get it right? I mean, what was going on there? Do you know?

Mr. Kennedy. Mr. Cummings, we were gathering information. We were closely coordinating with our colleagues in the intelligence community.

We wanted to know what was happening more than anyone else because we also had dozens of other embassies that we were concerned about, including attacks on three or four other embassies. So we were looking for every piece of information that we could get from no matter what rational and reasonable source to feed into our consideration of what steps we should take to protect U.S. Diplomatic facilities abroad.

Mr. Cummings. Just one last question, Mr. Chairman.

Is it unusual for you all to rely on the intelligence community for that kind of information?

Mr. Kennedy. We have a great partnership, Mr. Cummings, with the intelligence community, and we heavily depend upon the information they provide us, just as they heavily depend upon the information we provide them.

Mr. Cummings. Thank you, Mr. Chairman.

Chairman Issa. I thank you.

And now the gentleman from Ohio has exactly 5 minutes.

Mr. Jordan. Thank you. I thank the chairman.

Lieutenant Colonel Wood, how many months were you in Libya?

Colonel Wood. I was in Libya approximately 6 months.

Mr. Jordan. Mr. Nordstrom, how many months were you in Libya?

Mr. Nordstrom. Approximately 10.

Mr. Jordan. Ms. Lamb, how many times have you visited Libya in the--how many times have you visited Libya, period?

Ms. Lamb. I have not.

Mr. Jordan. None over the last 14, 15 months?

Ms. Lamb. No.

Mr. Jordan. None since the 200-plus incidents, security incidents, in Libya you have visited?

Ms. Lamb. No, sir.

Mr. Jordan. Mr. Kennedy, how many times have you been to Libya?

Mr. Kennedy. None.

Mr. Jordan. Okay.

Let me go to this process. We had numbers earlier from Mr. Nordstrom. You talked about three/five in Libya. Then we talked about you wanted 12, plus a backup of 6. So I want to know about this process. And, actually, I will go to Mr. Kennedy first.

In your testimony, Mr. Kennedy, you say, ``The Department of State regularly assesses risk in allocation of resources for security, a process which involves considered judgments of experienced professionals on the ground and in Washington using the best information available.''

So that process, I want to know how the decision was made. Are you involved in that process, Ambassador Kennedy?

Mr. Kennedy. In most normal occasions I am not involved. There is an ongoing dialogue----

Mr. Jordan. Where does that process go to? Are people in the White House directly involved in that process? Is Secretary Clinton directly involved in that process?

Mr. Kennedy. The process--if there are disagreements between the post in the field and the diplomatic security----

Mr. Jordan. Would you classify what took place here as a disagreement, based on what Mr. Nordstrom and Mr. Wood have testified to and what Ms. Lamb has said?

Mr. Kennedy. No, sir. I would----

Mr. Jordan. This didn't reach the disagreement level?

Mr. Kennedy. I would describe it as a dialogue between the post and diplomatic security----

Mr. Jordan. So this didn't reach a level where you needed to weigh in or someone higher needed to weigh in?

Mr. Kennedy. No, sir, it did not.

Mr. Jordan. Anyone at the National Security Council, did anyone weigh in there?

Mr. Kennedy. No, sir, it did not.

Mr. Jordan. Okay.

Mr. Nordstrom, let me turn to you then. I want to know, in the email that Congressman Chaffetz referenced earlier, the interview you had with Congressman Chaffetz and Chairman Issa back on October 1st, you stated, quote, ``This is not an environment where posts should be directed to normalize operations and reduce security resources in accordance with artificial timelines.''

And yet today in your testimony it was a little different tenor, as I think the ranking member brought out. And you mentioned at one point, the answer should not be to operate from a bunker. So I want to ask you these questions.

First of all, since that interview with Chairman Issa and Chairman Chaffetz, staff has indicated they have tried to contact you six different times via telephone and you have not responded. Is there a reason you did not respond to those telephone calls?

Mr. Nordstrom. That is correct----

Mr. Jordan. No, it is correct you didn't respond. Is there a reason?

Mr. Nordstrom. I had been advised by the Department of State that all inquiries----

Mr. Jordan. And who specifically advised you to do that?

Mr. Nordstrom. Our legislative affairs office.

Mr. Jordan. And did they say where that came from? Did Ms. Lamb specifically advise you not to talk?

Mr. Nordstrom. No, she did not.

Mr. Jordan. Did Ambassador Kennedy tell you to do that?

Mr. Nordstrom. No, he did not.

Mr. Jordan. Did Secretary of State Clinton tell you to do that?

Mr. Nordstrom. No, she did not.

Mr. Jordan. So who was the person who told you not to talk with our staff after you gave us this interview where you gave us this information?

Mr. Nordstrom. I was advised by the Assistant Secretary Boswell----

Mr. Jordan. Okay.

Mr. Nordstrom. --by his office, his staff that all requests for information and documents would need to go--would need to be vetted or routed through that office.

Mr. Jordan. Did those same individuals help you prepare today's testimony?

Mr. Nordstrom. In the sense of providing general guidelines on how----

Mr. Jordan. Did they tell you they wanted to look it over before you came in front of this committee and gave it today?

Mr. Nordstrom. Of course.

Mr. Jordan. And did they write it for you?

Mr. Nordstrom. No, they did not.

Mr. Jordan. Okay.

Ms. Lamb, I want to go back to--I want to go back to this decision-making process. So is it customary to not listen as--well, I would characterize it as listen as intently as I think you should to the guys in the field and what they wanted to have happen when they requested the 12 plus the 6 backup?

Ms. Lamb. Yes, sir, I listened intently to those conversations.

Mr. Jordan. Okay.

Mr. Wood, let me bring you into the conversation here. I want your comments on that, specifically the number you wanted to add in Libya, plus the additional six.

Colonel Wood. We agreed to the numbers, between Eric and I, and put forth those numbers. We felt great frustration in the fact that those demands were ignored or in some cases just never met.

Mr. Jordan. So the process I was earlier referencing when asking Ambassador Kennedy, tell me who you felt was involved in that process? Who were the individuals in Washington? You were the folks on the ground, at post. Who were the folks in Washington in that process?

Mr. Wood. I heard Eric Nordstrom refer to Ms. Lamb, as far as the deciding authority on providing those additional resources.

Mr. Jordan. Experienced professionals on the ground in Washington. Who were the other experienced professionals in Washington that helped make that decision?

Colonel Wood. I wouldn't know the answer to that.

Mr. Jordan. Mr. Nordstrom, who else?

Because all we got right now, we know the Secretary of State wasn't, we know the White House wasn't, and we know the National Security--and we know Ambassador Kennedy wasn't. Somebody had to decide. Someone in Washington was telling you guys you couldn't get what you wanted. So was it just Ms. Lamb, or were there other people involved in this process?

Mr. Nordstrom?

Mr. Nordstrom. Again, I can't speculate in terms of who was. The person I dealt with was our regional director, Jim Bacigalupo, and then Ms. Lamb. The----

Mr. Jordan. Okay----

Mr. Nordstrom. The Ambassador and the DCM, if I could just add----

Chairman Issa. Okay, you can finish----

Mr. Nordstrom. --raised the same concerns. The DCM met with DAS Lamb also in February, raised the same concerns in person. And it is my understanding that Ambassador Cretz made additional phone calls. All of us at post were in sync that we wanted these resources.

Mr. Jordan. Okay.

Chairman Issa. Okay. Anyone that needs to answer that question, but the gentleman's time has expired. Ms. Lamb?

On behalf of Ms. Lamb, Ambassador Kennedy.

Mr. Kennedy. Because I want to make----

Briefly, please.

Mr. Kennedy. Absolutely, Mr. Chairman.

I was asked--on a different question, I was asked whether I was going to request a third extension of the SST. I consulted with my colleagues, and because our colleagues had put together----

Mr. Jordan. Wait, but that is not what you said earlier. You said you weren't involved, and now you are telling me you are. Which one is it?

Mr. Kennedy. This is a--you asked a specific question----

Chairman Issa. Okay. This question, I am afraid, will be for the next round for both of you.

With that, we recognize the gentleman from Ohio also, Mr. Kucinich.

Mr. Kucinich. Thank you very much, Mr. Chairman.

Mr. Kennedy has testified today that U.S. interests and values are at stake in Libya and that the U.S. is better off because we went to Benghazi. Really? You would think that after 10 years in Iraq and 11 years in Afghanistan, that our country, that the U.S. would have learned the consequences and the limits of interventionism. You would think that after trillions have been wasted on failed attempts at democracy-building abroad while our infrastructure crumbles at home, Congress and the administration would reexamine priorities.

Today we are engaging in a discussion about the security failures in Benghazi. There was a security failure. Four Americans, including our Ambassador, Ambassador Christopher Stevens, were killed. Their deaths are a national tragedy, and my sympathy is with the families of those who were killed. There has to be accountability, and I haven't heard that yet. We have an obligation to protect those who protect us. That is why this Congress needs to ask questions.

The security situation did not happen overnight because of a decision made by someone at the State Department. We could talk about hundreds of millions of dollars in cuts for funding for embassy security over the last 2 years as a result of a blind pursuit of fiscal austerity. We could talk about whether it is prudent to rely so heavily on security contractors rather than our own military or State Department personnel. We could do a he-said/she-said about whether the State Department should have beefed up security at the Embassy in Benghazi. But we owe it to the diplomatic corps who serves our Nation to start at the beginning, and that is what I shall do.

The security threats in Libya, including the unchecked extremist groups who are armed to the teeth, exist because our Nation spurred on a civil war, destroying the security and stability of Libya. And, you know, no one defends Qadhafi. Libya was not in a meltdown before the war. In 2003, Qadhafi reconciled with the community of nations by giving up his nation's pursuit of nuclear weapons. At the time, President Bush said Qadhafi's actions made our country and our world safer.

Now, during the Arab Spring, uprisings across the Middle East occurred, and Qadhafi made ludicrous threats against Benghazi. Based on those verbal threats, we intervened--absent constitutional authority, I might add. We bombed Libya, we destroyed their army, we obliterated their police stations. Lacking any civil authority, armed brigades controlled security. Al Qaeda expanded its presence. Weapons are everywhere. Thousands of shoulder-to-air missiles are on the loose.

Our military intervention led to greater instability in Libya. Many of us, Democrats and Republicans alike, made that argument to try to stop the war. It is not surprising, given the inflated threat and the grandiose expectations inherent in our nation-building in Libya, that the State Department was not able to adequately protect our diplomats from this predictable threat. It is not surprising, and it is also not acceptable.

It is easy to blame someone else, like a civil servant at the State Department. We all know the game. It is harder to acknowledge that decades of American foreign policy have directly contributed to regional instability and the rise of armed militias around the world.

It is even harder to acknowledge Congress's role in the failure to stop the war in Libya, the war in Iraq, the war in Afghanistan, the war in Pakistan, the war in Yemen, the war in Somalia, and who knows where else. It is harder to recognize Congress's role in the failure to stop the drone attacks that are still killing innocent civilians and strengthening radical elements abroad.

We want to stop the attacks on our embassies? Let's stop trying to overthrow governments. This should not be a partisan issue. Let's avoid the hype. Let's look at the real situation here. Interventions do not make us safer. They do not protect our Nation. They are, themselves, a threat to America.

Now, Mr. Kennedy, I would like to ask you, is al Qaeda more or less established in Libya since our involvement?

Mr. Kennedy. Mr. Kucinich, I will have to take that question for the record. I am not an intelligence expert.

Mr. Kucinich. Oh, you don't have the intelligence, you are saying. Well, I am going to go on to the next question.

The next question: Are Americans safer, Mr. Kennedy----

Chairman Issa. Mr. Kucinich?

Mr. Kucinich. Excuse me?

Chairman Issa. I think the other two may have an opinion, also, if you wanted to ask them about that.

Mr. Kucinich. Well, I wanted to ask Ambassador Kennedy.

Next question, Ambassador Kennedy: How many shoulder-to-air missiles are capable of shooting--that are capable of shooting down civilian passenger airlines are still missing in Libya? And this happened since our intervention. Can you answer that question?

Mr. Kennedy. No, sir. I will be glad to provide it for the record.

Mr. Kucinich. You are saying that you don't know.

Mr. Kennedy. I do not know, sir. It is not within my normal purview of operations at the State Department.

Mr. Kucinich. Does anyone else here know how many shoulder-to-air missiles that can shoot down civilian airliners are still loose in Libya? Does anyone know?

Mr. Nordstrom. The figures that we were provided were fluid, but the rough approximation was between 10,000 and 20,000.

Chairman Issa. The gentleman's time has expired. Did you want them to answer anything about al Qaeda growth?

Mr. Kucinich. If anyone there knows the answer.

Chairman Issa. If anyone has an answer on that one, they can answer, and then we will move on.

Mr. Kucinich. Yeah. Is al Qaeda more or less established in Libya since our involvement?

Colonel Wood. Yes, sir, and their presence grows every day. They are certainly more established than we are.

Chairman Issa. Thank you.

With that, we recognize the chairman of the subcommittee and a doggedly determined individual to get to the bottom of this, Mr. Chaffetz.

Mr. Chaffetz. Thank you, Mr. Chairman.

Mr. Nordstrom, as we spoke before and I think is clear in the record, you were asking for more personnel and that was either rejected or denied or just simply ignored, correct?

Mr. Nordstrom. Actually, to clarify, we were asking just to keep what we had.

Mr. Chaffetz. And when you weren't able to just even keep what you had, what happened to your pay and the other security officers' on the ground?

Mr. Nordstrom. I am sorry, I----

Mr. Chaffetz. As I recall, what you told me is, when that was denied, you were given a pay increase. They increased your pay.

Mr. Nordstrom. Ah, okay. What I think you are referring to is the increase in danger pay for post. As part of normal procedures, we are asked for input at post. I, as part of that process, would provide information on security----

Mr. Chaffetz. So, to clarify, you were asking for more assets, more resources, more personnel; that was denied. But the State Department went back and reclassified it as more dangerous. The danger pay, therefore, increased. They didn't tell you that we didn't have resources, hey, that Congress just cut your budget. They gave you an increase because the danger was rising, correct?

Mr. Nordstrom. That is correct. We received a danger pay increase.

Mr. Chaffetz. Thank you.

Did the buildings in Benghazi meet the so-called Inman standards? After the bombings in Beirut, we went back as a government and formalized some minimum standards. Did they or did they not meet those minimum standards?

Mr. Nordstrom. Neither the buildings in Benghazi nor the buildings in Tripoli met those standards, nor was there a plan for the next phase of construction, what was called the interim embassy, would they meet the standards either. That interim embassy was scheduled to be on the ground for approximately 10 years. That was a major cause of concern, and that was the main physical security issue that we continued to raise.

Mr. Chaffetz. Thank you.

And, Mr. Chairman, I would point to an August 20 cable, that U.N. Officials believe the Supreme Security Council is, quote, ``fading away,'' unquote, unwilling to take on, quote, ``anyone with powerful patrons or from powerful tribes,'' end quote. This cable back to Washington, D.C., also said that incidents continue in this ``security vacuum,'' as they referred to it, in Benghazi.

Mr. Chairman, I would also point to September 4th. In their memo, they highlighted the September 1st, quote, ``maximum alert''--a maximum alert, September 1st. This was the information that was coming.

And what is infuriating is that we have hundreds of terrorist types of activities. Our consulate is bombed twice. The British Ambassador has an assassination attempt. And you are over here arguing about whether the number was five or two, or five or three. And the security experts who actually have even been to Libya didn't get the resources that they asked for.

Colonel Wood, did you participate in any way, shape, or form in requests for additional personnel in Libya? And what was the consequence of those requests?

Colonel Wood. Yes, sir, I did. I assisted Eric Nordstrom in preparation of the requests for support. Inasmuch as they dealt with SST support, I reviewed some of those documents and assisted in the preparation of those.

I would like to add also that there was frustration from the beginning. The initial, or perhaps it was the second request for extension that occurred on April 5th, Ambassador Cretz encountered some difficulty in understanding what was going on. He was getting conflicting signals from DOD and DOS. I got him together with General Ham. They worked out a complete understanding, and General Ham made it very clear to Ambassador Cretz that he could have the SST as long as he needed them. This was a great interagency cooperation, and that was made very clear to him.

It was also made clear to Joan Polaschik, who took over as charge d'affaires in between Ambassador Cretz and Ambassador Stevens. He came personally and told her that.

He also had a VTC with Ambassador Stevens and reiterated that same point, that the SST was his as long he needed them. All he had to do was request them, and General Ham was perfectly willing to provide that support.

Mr. Chaffetz. Mr. Nordstrom, did you ever specifically ask Charlene Lamb--rather, did she ever specifically direct you not to ask for additional DOD SST extension?

Mr. Nordstrom. I recall two specific phone calls, one in the February timeframe, one in the July timeframe. I had the opportunity to refresh my recollection on one of those phone calls by talking to the two agents who happened to be present in the living room of the Ambassador's residence, which is where we used as our office.

In those conversations, I recall that I was specifically told you cannot request an SST extension. How I interpreted that was that there was going to be too much political cost, or for some reason, there was hesitancy on that. In the first case, in February, the Ambassador and DCM and I all felt strongly about the need for that. And we went ahead and requested it anyway.

Mr. Chaffetz. Thank you, Mr. Chairman.

Chairman Issa. Thank you. Thank you.

We now go to the gentleman from Massachusetts--and we appreciate his patience--for 5 minutes.

Mr. Lynch. Thank you, Mr. Chairman. I also want to thank the witnesses, all of you, for your willingness to come and help the committee with its work. Obviously, I want to acknowledge the tremendous sacrifice of Ambassador Stevens and former Navy SEALs Tyrone Woods and Glen Doherty, who was a favorite son of Massachusetts, my home State, and as well as Communications Specialist Sean Smith.

I want to make two points, however. One is, I think the best way to honor the memory of those American heroes is to address the general and global issue of embassy security so that when we do assign other brave Americans to fill these posts, that they do have adequate security.

Now many members of this committee, both sides of the aisle here, have traveled to the Middle East dozens and dozens of times. We have visited some--and the chairman has mentioned them in his opening remarks--mentioned Damascus; Syria; mentioned Beirut, Lebanon. I just came back from Sana'a, Yemen, where at least in Yemen, they are undergoing some structural changes there in response to threats there. But we have some embassies that predate even the attacks on Nairobi, Kenya, or Dar es Salaam, Tanzania, so that we have got old-world embassies that are located right on the street, right on the souk in the Middle East that are terribly exposed to car bombs and to attacks.

So I think the best way really to approach this thing is, number one, is take a holistic approach to this and figure out how we can prevent this type of thing from happening again.

And I think my second point, really, the easiest way to strengthen embassy security is to get on the same page. I have to tell it like it is. And in recent budgets, my Republican colleagues have supported cuts to funding for embassy security. Well, the first thing you have got to do to strengthen embassy security is to try to meet Secretary Clinton's request for funding for embassy security. That will help a lot.

Ambassador Kennedy and Ms. Lamb, what would a few hundred million dollars, like was cut from the President's request and Secretary Clinton's request for embassy security, what would that mean to you in terms of providing that level of protection that every son and daughter of America deserves when they accept that post to go into a dangerous area, especially some of the spots that we have got right now in the Middle East, what would that few hundred million dollars do to your ability to provide an adequate level of protection on their behalf?

Mr. Kennedy. Mr. Lynch, if we received the President's budget request for fiscal year 2013, which is still pending before the Congress, we would be able to construct new facilities and we would be able to upgrade additional facilities to get to the higher standards we seek.

Mr. Lynch. Well, look, I want to go back to the Chairman's point, the situations in Damascus and in Beirut. Obviously, Damascus we have withdrawn our embassy personnel. But we have still got the same problem there when things get straightened out. We are still on the main street. We are negotiating--we were negotiating. I had personal conversations with President Assad a couple of years ago about getting a new facility there.

Do we have a task force that is looking at providing the setback we need to provide that level of protection and to relocate some of these embassies?

Mr. Kennedy. We do, sir. We have a strategic plan. We know which embassies are more in danger than others. We are working through that. But there are limitations on funds. I can only construct so many new facilities each year, depending on the funds I have available to me.

Mr. Lynch. I just want to go back to one point, Ms. Lamb. In your written testimony at page 2, first paragraph, you mention that in addition to the security team you had there, there was, I think you described it as a rapid response force that was located in the annex. How many folks are in that rapid, do you know? How many are in that rapid response task force or team that would help? Or, Mr. Nordstrom, I don't know if you know the number of that.

Ms. Lamb. Sir, there were seven. And their job was also to hook up with----

Mr. Chaffetz. Point of order. Point of order.

Chairman Issa. The gentleman will state his point of order.

Mr. Chaffetz. Again, I would renew my deep concern that we are getting into an area that is classified--and should be classified. The dealing with the map is one issue. I believe that the markings on that map were terribly inappropriate. But the activities there could cost lives.

Mr. Lynch. On the point of order--may I speak on the point of order?

Chairman Issa. You may speak on the point of order, of course.

Mr. Lynch. Okay.

This whole hearing is responding to allegations that there were not enough people on the ground at the Benghazi facility, those accusations that you made publicly, so that now I am trying to get an answer of how many people were there, and all of a sudden that is off the record, that is classified information? You have got to be kidding me. You have got to be kidding me.

Chairman Issa. I am prepared to rule.

Unless you are prepared to get clearance to declassify any and all information about additional personnel, this hearing will be limited to the information already given, which is the amount of individuals who responded from that rapid force. This hearing is not specifically about September 11, but it is intended to clarify much more prospectively failures, accountability decisions. I don't think that any of us--and I don't want to overly state this--but I don't think any of us figure since four people are dead, something went wrong. Having said that, there has previously been testimony as to the individuals that have responded.

I would certainly recommend the entire committee have a classified briefing as to any and all other assets that were not drawn upon but could have been drawn upon. And I would ask the gentleman to respect that. And I would yield the gentleman an additional 1 minute to finish his questioning.

Mr. Lynch. Okay. Mr. Ambassador, can you clarify any answer around that question that may not violate----

Mr. Kennedy. Certainly, sir. The U.S. mission, the American embassy annexes in Benghazi consisted of two separate compounds because we could not all fit on one compound. There were security personnel stationed on both compounds. There was an affected type of mutual assistance arrangement that had been worked out by the regional security officers, so if one compound came under attack, security personnel would flow from one to the other or vice versa. It is a common practice. And so we are very, very interested in making sure that we have the maximum utilization for common U.S. Government-State Department security personnel in any country, and we do that. And we are certainly mindful and respectful of the general security concerns.

Mr. Lynch. Thank you. I yield back.

Chairman Issa. I thank the gentleman.

Only one point of clarification. Mr. Nordstrom, during your time were those people under any of your control or could you task them?

Mr. Nordstrom. I am glad you asked that question. Again, in being completely cognizant, because I have some of the same concerns, all of the people there were under the Chief of Mission. But not necessarily all of the security people fell under my direct operational control.

Chairman Issa. Thank you. I think that clarifies it. We now go to the gentleman from Oklahoma, Mr. Lankford, for 5 minutes.

Mr. Lankford. Thank you, Mr. Chairman. I need to shift my questions a little bit from what I intended just based on some of the conversation that we have had so far.

Ms. Lamb, can you clarify for me, where were you working September 11th? Were you in the Washington area or in the main facility there?

Ms. Lamb. Yes, sir. I was in the DS Command Center on the evening of the event.

Mr. Lankford. You note that in your testimony, that you are in the diplomatic security command center, and then you make this statement: I could follow what was happening almost in real-time.

Ms. Lamb. That is correct.

Mr. Lankford. So once they hit the button in Benghazi you are alerted. It said you could have. Did you follow what was happening in real-time at that point?

Ms. Lamb. Sir, what was happening is they were making multiple phone calls and it was very important that they communicate with the annex in Tripoli because this is where additional resources were coming from. So they would hang up on us and then call back.

Mr. Lankford. But you are tracking it back and forth, what is going on.

Ms. Lamb. Yes.

Mr. Lankford. Then, after a very long night for them, they are evacuated out into Tripoli. Where they in communication with you then once they got to Tripoli? This would have been the next morning at that point.

Ms. Lamb. No. At that point Embassy Tripoli took over communicating.

Mr. Lankford. So you had no other communication with them after they got to Tripoli. You weren't aware of that or----

Ms. Lamb. No. They notified us when there was wheels down. They notified us when they got to the hospital. They notified us when they were wheels up in route to Germany.

Mr. Lankford. Obviously, these are your folks. I cannot imagine the emotion of that for you. So you had no other connection to know what happened, the details of that, what occurred. These frantic phone calls and all these things that are happening back and forth, they get to Tripoli and you are not aware any more of what actually had just happened?

Ms. Lamb. No, sir, we continued to follow them, but half the team had to be rushed to the hospital----

Mr. Lankford. Right.

Ms. Lamb. And treated. They had just been through a horrific ordeal.

Mr. Lankford. Oh, it is horrible. Your detailed account of this is horrific.

Ms. Lamb. So at this point, providing them the comfort to just come down from the adrenaline and the horror of what had happened, we respected that and we worked through our colleagues at the embassy in Tripoli.

Mr. Lankford. Right. Here is my struggle with that. You are listening in on the command center. You are in communication as this is going on. They get to Tripoli. There is all kinds of conversations that are happening back and forth as people are checking on them. And yet State Department is testifying still today, 5 days later they didn't know what happened; that that was--a coordinated--maybe this was some spontaneous event that occurred, when there was constant communication happening.

Did someone come to you and ask you from State: Was this a protest? Because I would assume you knew pretty quickly this was not some protest that went out of bounds because there was no protest even there that day. So it is not like there is a big group of people and 24 people jumped out and started shooting. There was no gathering at all that day. I assume you knew that immediately.

Ms. Lamb. No, sir. It was not clear. It was a very large compound and each individual agent was looking at what was happening from a different perspective and a different angle.

Mr. Lankford. Was it clear to you there wasn't a protest going on outside? It is not that large of a compound you can't see out the front gates and know if there is a protest.

Ms. Lamb. No, sir. It happened so fast. When they rushed through the gate, it is was not clear.

Mr. Lankford. I completely understand; 9:40 at night. The initial reports were this was some large protest that had happened over a video and it kind of birthed out of that where people are running out with RPGs and had attacked. And Ambassador Kennedy said that is the best we would know even 5 days later. I find that hard to believe, based on your report that you are tracking what is occurring and that individuals, when they get to Tripoli the next morning are reporting back what happened, that someone didn't say: Here's what occurred. And the word ``protest'' never came out of it. And 5 days later no one knows?

Ms. Lamb. Sir, they were all fighting for their lives on that compound.

Mr. Lankford. I completely understand that. My question is: The testimony seems to be conflicting today. We are getting reports from State that--this wasn't them, this was the Intelligence Community that made this report, but I hear from you, you were aware of what happened and what went on and others around you, and folks at the embassy, I can't imagine 5, 6, 7--7 days later the White House press secretary standing up and still giving the same report 7 days later, that no one has done this.

Now there are lots of other issues I want to talk about, but I am kind of amazed at this whole dialogue today that it seems like no one knew and there is this best case scenario that is coming out. And I am struggling with just the basic facts on this. Now this is irrelevant to the overall of what we are going to do in the future and what happened in the past. But I can't seem to put all these pieces together when I am getting such conflicting stories of people that are listening to it firsthand what is happening on the ground.

Ambassador Kennedy, do you want to respond to that?

Mr. Kennedy. If I could, sir. There were multiple reports coming out. Multiple reports.

Mr. Lankford. Were any of the reports saying there was a protest?

Mr. Kennedy. There were reports.

Mr. Lankford. There were reports coming out of Benghazi that there were protests that day.

Mr. Kennedy. There were reports that we received saying that there were protests. And I will not go any farther than that. And then things evolved. Period.

If I could, one other thing.

Chairman Issa. Before the gentleman goes on, you said you wouldn't go any further. I would only ask why you are not going any further. If you want to revise and extend other things, that is fine, but why won't you go further?

Mr. Kennedy. Because I don't want to cross certain lines in open session.

Chairman Issa. Okay. So you are testifying there were multiple reports, but in this setting, you cannot tell us the multiple reports and where they came from?

Mr. Kennedy. In open session.

Chairman Issa. I appreciate that. We will arrange for a classified.

If the gentleman will conclude.

Mr. Lankford. Just my one issue is there is ongoing conversation happening, there is ongoing conversations the next morning when they are in Tripoli. I find it very difficult 5, 6, 7 days later this same story is coming out when there was constant communication with a group of people. It just seems like a very difficult story for me to be able to believe.

Mr. Kennedy. If I could.

Mr. Lankford. Of course.

Mr. Kennedy. As I said in my opening statement, Mr. Chairman, Mr. Lankford, there were multiple reports. We are trying to reconcile the reports. Because we regard our responsibility to keep the Congress informed, we came up very, very early to talk when we still had multiple threads out there. And those--we were not about to precipitously try to reconcile those multiple threads.

Chairman Issa. I appreciate that. And I do appreciate the fact that 2 days later you called it a terrorist attack; well, many days later others were using other terms.

As I pass over to the minority for a moment, yesterday in a closed session, I asked you for the 50-minute tape that exists that would allow us to see the video feed that was available. You said it wasn't available; another part of government had it, even though you had a copy of it. Have you been able to make that available? I think on both sides of this side of the dais, we would like to see that 50 minutes of video that was turned over by the government fairly quickly.

Mr. Kennedy. Mr. Chairman, I have made it clear to the other government agency that has this tape--I have communicated your request to them.

Chairman Issa. With your recommendations that they do turn it over?

Mr. Kennedy. Since this is involving investigative process on their part, I do not feel that I am in a position to make a recommendation about an investigative process.

Chairman Issa. Thank you. And for the ranking member's edification, I apologize that I only barely learned about that hearing, or that briefing in order to get there for a few minutes, so that I want to confirm, the FBI is doing the investigation. They do not have custody. Another government agency does. I don't have any doubt that it is not the investigating agency, the FBI that has custody of that tape.

Mr. Cummings. The same briefing that you are talking about, we were not--the Dems on the committee, we weren't invited. Didn't even know about it.

Chairman Issa. Your committee did know about it.

Mr. Cummings. But we weren't invited.

Were you invited?

Chairman Issa. I learned about it in a discussion with the Secretary of State. And so I went up there, only then discovering that they were surprised to see me. But I was glad I went there and I was glad to have the opportunity to confirm the existence of a 50-minute tape that has been floating around that is not needed by the FBI, but, in fact, is in the custody of another government agency.

Mr. Cummings. Mr. Chairman, one more thing. I think you would agree that we don't want to do anything to interfere with an ongoing investigation. Do we?

Chairman Issa. I would like this committee to have that 50-minute tape before the press has it. And quite frankly, we should have had it before today to see it. It is not interfering with an investigation. In testimony, the last 2 days that both of our committees had, we were told, for example, that when the wall was blown up some months earlier, they didn't see it blown up because they didn't have the video equipment to do it and it was pointed the wrong way. They told us they didn't have enough people to man the TOC, so they, in fact, were not there being able to pan and look for it. They told us they didn't have the people inside. And much of that, perhaps, is beyond the scope. But since people told us what assets they didn't have with specificity, and that will be in our report, yes, I would like to see what those tapes did discover.

Ms. Lamb told us that there was somebody monitoring the TOC. Quite frankly, we were talk that they slept there and there were not people to constantly be panning those cameras. So I have like to see when they began panning them, example. And there is multiple evidence that we haven't gotten. We are not going to get it here today. I just wanted to make sure that the State Department would be clear that they have no objections to us having it.

Mr. Cummings. Is that right, Mr. Kennedy?

Mr. Kennedy. Mr. Cummings, Mr. Chairman, we defer to the law enforcement investigative elements on this matter.

Chairman Issa. The FBI told me they don't have it and it is not theirs and they don't need it. So hopefully, you will stop using law enforcement, another part of government.

Thank you.

We now go to the very patient gentleman from Tennessee for 5 minutes.

Mr. Cooper. Thank you, Mr. Chairman. All Americans mourn the loss of the four brave Americans who died in Benghazi. It is important, I think, that we put their sacrifice, their tragedy in context; particularly, historical context. Serving America abroad is dangerous. And certainly every U.S. veteran knows that freedom is not free. Our State Department personnel know that too. But sometimes civilians comfortable here at home forget. And sometimes these terrible incidents are not covered as they should be. But sometimes we are focused on other things.

I would like to read an honor roll of the fallen from a previous time. These men, in some cases women, died as victims of terrorists. It was in a different time, when we had a great President, Ronald Reagan, who is particularly known for his strength on national defense.

I was only able to find a database of the Navy and marine victims. But there are 56 dead, 46 wounded. And a lot of us remember that as more or less a peaceful time. It was not. So let me read.

Master Bosanmate Sam Novello, killed by Turkish leftists, Istanbul, Turkey; three marines wounded in a terrorist attack in Costa Rica; one crewman killed, three wounded from the USS Pensacola, attacked by terrorists in San Juan, Puerto, Rico; one U.S. embassy marine security guard wounded, Beirut, Lebanon; terrorist bombing of the U.S. Embassy in Beirut, Lebanon; Lieutenant Commander Albert A. Schaufelberger, killed by terrorists, San Salvador, El Salvador; Corporal Guillermo San Pedro, killed in a terrorist attack in Cyprus; Captain George Tsantes, shot by terrorists near Athens, Greece; Lieutenant Corporal Rudolfo Hernandez, killed in a terrorist attack, Germany; Hospitalman Carl P. Englund, wounded, Beirut, Lebanon; Petty Officer First Class Michael R. Wagner, assigned to the Defense Attache Office, killed; Civil Engineer Corps Builder Harvey L. Whitaker, killed; Builder First Class Steven E. Haycock and four marine security guards wounded in terrorist bombing of U.S. Embassy Annex, East Beirut, Lebanon.

Seabees. Steelworker Second Class Robert Dean Stethem of Underwater Construction Team One, killed by terrorists, Athens, Greece; Off-duty marines assigned to Marine Security Guard Detachment, San Salvador, killed by terrorists armed with automatic weapons at a cafe in San Salvador; 37 killed, 5 wounded when the USS Stark was struck by Iraqi missiles, Persian Gulf; terrorist grenade attack at the USO Club in Barcelona, Spain.

Colonel Rich Higgins, killed by two pro-Iranian terrorists; USS Samuel B. Roberts struck by an Iranian mine, Persian Gulf; Japanese Red Army terrorist bombing of the USO Club in Naples, Italy; loss of an attack helicopter during operations against Iranian naval forces; and Captain William E. Nordeen, Defense and Naval Attache, killed by terrorist car bomb, Athens, Greece.

And that was just during one administration of a President known for his strong defense policy.

So we should be thankful for the sacrifice of our men and women abroad. As you pointed out, Ms. Lamb, you are in charge of 275 posts around the world. Too many Americans can't find these places on a map, much less appreciate the sacrifice and the risks involved of serving in many lawless zones.

So I appreciate Lieutenant Colonel Wood and Mr. Nordstrom in particular for helping supervise our security needs in these posts, because the dangers are incredible, especially when we can live in comfort here at home. So thank you for your service and sacrifice.

Mr. Burton. The gentleman's time has expired. The chair recognizes Mr. Gosar of Arizona.

Mr. Gosar. Thank you, Mr. Chairman. First of all, my family would like to honor the memory of our fellow patriots that loss their lives in this senseless and preventable act of violence committed in Benghazi on September 11th, a day that will forever be regarded as a day of unity for American citizens--and a warning. And with that, I am going to come back.

In an interview with the committee yesterday, Ms. Lamb said that in May, 2012, Embassy Tripoli had come back and said things were going so great, the RSO gave up 6 of the 16 SSTs. I just assume that if the RSO, Nordstrom, was willing to give up assets and not ask for replacements, that he didn't need them. But, again, the functions that they were being used for were being slowly filled by local national employees.

Lieutenant Wood, is it true in your time in Libya that things were going that great, and would you describe the conditions in Libya from your personal point of view?

Colonel Wood. Yes, sir. From my personal point of view, things in Libya always remained difficult and uncertain and could devolve at any moment into further problems and result in loss of life almost at any minute. SST members were fully integrated with the diplomatic security people there and worked through and under all these difficult circumstances.

I have a couple of things here I am trying to find.

There were numerous incidents. Lawless situation was pretty much the norm. There was assassinations that went on of Qadhafi loyalists. And back and forth. Insurgent activity continued along the border town of Al Kufra, where it drained a lot of the meager resources of the fledgling government to go down there and try to put down rebellious and insurgent activity going on down there. There was no control of the borders or weapons smuggling in or out of the country. There was a loss of control of weapons types previously mentioned here--the shoulder-fired missiles. And tanks and anti-aircraft guns could be found in the possession of almost anyone anywhere in Libya. Tribal interests frequently competed with each other and resulted in fire fights. It was a common occurrence.

When I first arrived on the ground in Tripoli, I got to where I could recognize celebratory gunfire from actual

gunfire fights. They were shooting at each other. That did die off a little bit. However, we did notice an increase in targeted attacks towards Americans. These indicators spelled out to me that the country was far from secure and that the

SST, as it had been originally conceived, was still in need at that location.

Mr. Gosar. Well, in a document that was produced in late July--and I have that document right here. The document is over 230 events in Libya since June of 2011. Mr. Nordstrom included this in his part of the general assessment on the security environment. In fact, prior to this attack on our embassy, didn't the Red Cross and the British consulate move out of Libya?

Colonel Wood. Yes, sir, that is entirely correct. The British consulate moved out when I was there and they actually had an MOU with us to leave their weapons and vehicles on our compound there in Benghazi. They would come back and occupy at times, draw their weapons and vehicles, and do their work, and return them and leave.

The attack on the International Red Cross was another attack that also involved us and threats to the compound there in Benghazi. The threats were made on Facebook to both the remaining Western influences there in Benghazi, being the Red Cross and the U.S. Embassy compound. The Red Cross was attacked with rocket-propelled grenades in early June. When it was attacked a second time, I believe they made the decision they were going to give up and leave Benghazi. When that occurred, it was apparent to me that we were the last flag flying in Benghazi. We were the last thing on their target list to remove from Benghazi.

I voiced my concerns at the country team meeting. Although it was a difficult thing, the country team was left with no options at that point to try and change the security profile there in Benghazi. The resources had been withdrawn. The decision to not renew the SST was pretty much a foregone conclusion by that point in time, but I urged them to do something and anything, to include withdrawal from Benghazi, although I knew that was impossible at the time.

Mr. Gosar. Thank you, Mr. Chairman.

Chairman Issa. Would the gentleman yield to me?

Mr. Gosar. I would happily yield to the chairman.

Chairman Issa. Colonel Wood, you weren't there on September 11. Mr. Nordstrom, you weren't there on September 11. My understanding is several Americans successfully got out alive. The three armed individuals who represented Libyan nationals survived. From your experience, from your combat experience, from your training, both of you, what is the marginal difference between everybody getting out and half or so getting out? In other words, the State Department has been saying effectively nothing could have stopped this, this was so overwhelming. My question is: What would it take? Would one more armed agent have made a difference that everyone would have gotten out? Would two more, three more? I understand we will never know for sure, but what is the difference between chaos and control in a fire fight? Colonel Wood?

Colonel Wood. Superior weapons and superior tactics. That is what the SST brought to the table. Those were the qualities and attributes and the bolstering effect that they added to diplomatic security in this type of environment. When they were on the ground, those resident qualities were there for the use of the RSO. And when we left, they were no longer available as a possible resource.

Chairman Issa. Mr. Nordstrom, you would agree; that if it became necessary.

Mr. Nordstrom. Absolutely. In Tripoli, where we had--with the SST, I was never concerned that we would be able to repel any sort of assault there with the 16 and the additional DS agents.

Chairman Issa. Thank you. We now go to Mr. Connolly.

Mr. Cummings. Mr. Chairman, I ask unanimous consent for 1 minute. You went 2-1/2 minutes over. Just a minute and a half.

Chairman Issa. Would the gentleman from Virginia yield--I would ask unanimous consent the gentleman from Virginia has 6 minutes. Would the gentleman from Virginia consider yielding to the ranking member?

Mr. Connolly. I was hoping that the chairman was going to say that he asked unanimous consent to give a minute and a half to the ranking member. And I gladly would wait for that request, sir, and support it.

Chairman Issa. Take what you get.

Without objection, so ordered. Six minutes.

Mr. Cummings. Thank you. The gentleman yields. Thank you very much.

I just want to go back to something that you wrote in your statement, Mr. Nordstrom, in reference to the question that the chairman just asked you. And I quote you. I am reading from page 2. You said, ``Having an extra foot of wall or extra half dozen guards or agents would not have enabled us to respond to that kind of assault.''

Did you write that?

Mr. Nordstrom. Yes, I did. And I still believe that.

Mr. Cummings. Thank you.

Mr. Connolly. Thank you, Mr. Chairman. And thank you to the ranking member. I just want to say, picking up on my friend from

Tennessee's remarks, I was a young professional staff member in the Senate Foreign Relations Committee in the early 1980s when Ronald Reagan was in the White House and our marine amphibious unit was attacked by a truck bomb at the Beirut airport and dozens and dozens of young Americans were killed.

I had just been to Beirut on a Senate staff study, and shortly after I returned, our embassy was bombed in downtown Beirut, killing many more Americans, including a good friend of mine who worked at that time for USAID.

It is very serious business when tragedies occur in a dangerous world. To attempt to exploit it politically--and I know we are not trying to do that here, 27 days out from the election.

Colonel Wood, you testified that you had concerns and you approached--you are with the Utah National Guard, is that correct?

Colonel Wood. Yes, sir.

Mr. Connolly. And you approached your Congressperson with these concerns. I assume that is our colleague, Mr. Chaffetz?

Colonel Wood. Yes, sir. Initially, I tried to make contact with Senator McCain, because he had made several visits to Tripoli. I was unable to get a response from his office.

Mr. Connolly. I thank you. And about what time did you approach your Congressperson with these concerns?

Colonel Wood. I sent an email on Sunday, I believe it was the 28th of September.

Mr. Connolly. Of September. So fairly recently?

Colonel Wood. Yes, sir.

Mr. Connolly. Are you aware of the fact that the Democratic side of this aisle made several attempts, including an email to you last weekend, to try to contact you and to have some opportunity to explore with you the nature of those concerns you shared with Mr. Chaffetz, and possibly to understand what you might be testifying to today--a common, by the way, practice?

Colonel Wood. Yes, sir. I assumed that the information I was giving would be shared to the whole committee at some point. I wasn't sure when.

Mr. Connolly. So that is why you did not respond to the emails from Democratic staff members?

Colonel Wood. Yes, sir.

Mr. Connolly. You weren't, in any way, to pick up on Mr. Jordan's questioning of, or others on the panel, you weren't in any way encouraged or discouraged from talking to the Democratic side of the aisle in preparation for this hearing?

Colonel Wood. No, sir. It was simply easier for me to talk to one point of contact. With everything else I had going on, it was just easier to do.

Mr. Connolly. I thank you.

Ambassador Kennedy, is there an ongoing investigation into what occurred in Benghazi?

Mr. Kennedy. Yes, Mr. Connolly, there are actually two ongoing investigations, one being conducted by the Federal Bureau of Investigation, and another being conducted by the Accountability Review Board, which is a congressionally-mandated process that comes into being after a tragedy of this nature.

Mr. Connolly. And when do we expect those investigations to be completed and a report provided?

Mr. Kennedy. I cannot speak to the FBI investigation, sir. That is beyond my kin. But I know that the Secretary has asked the Accountability Review Board to proceed as expeditiously as possible while making sure that they are thorough and accurate.

Mr. Connolly. So we are having this hearing as those investigations have not completed their work or provided their findings?

Mr. Kennedy. That is correct, sir.

Mr. Connolly. I see. One of the things, if I am understanding, is it is awfully hard for me and others, I think, to follow what we are trying to get at here. Would you agree, Mr. Nordstrom, that certainly the Libya I experienced briefly--I was in Libya about the same amount of time I believe our colleague Mr. Chaffetz was, and I don't know, did he go to Benghazi? I don't think he went to Benghazi. Did you, Mr. Chaffetz?

Mr. Chaffetz. No. I was not allowed to go.

Mr. Connolly. Right. He and I both went to Tripoli. I was there in May. And it seemed a very volatile situation in terms of too many people with too many weapons, lots of militia, trying to keep control over who was a good guy and who was a bad guy. No matter how many security personnel we might have had in the field, that was a problem at that time, and I gather is still. Would that be an accurate assessment, Mr. Nordstrom.

Mr. Nordstrom. It was. That was one of our main struggles, just trying to figure out who was who.

Mr. Connolly. Right. And so inherently unstable as we are trying to transition from Qadhafi to something we hope is more democratic--a lot more democratic and more stable. Fair?

Mr. Nordstrom. Correct.

Mr. Connolly. Okay. Ambassador Kennedy described it not so much as a dispute as we are going back and forth about needs assessment. And it was your recommendation that the site security team be extended a third time, is that correct?

Mr. Nordstrom. That is correct.

Mr. Connolly. And, Mr. Ambassador, your view was, or your colleagues' view was actually we are trying to graduate from that. And we think we have got the assets to do that. Therefore, for whatever reason, that request was not honored because it was felt that it wasn't needed or what?

Mr. Kennedy. Mr. Connolly, what we were trying to do is build in a State Department capacity to replace the personnel we had borrowed from the Department of Defense. The SST was great. We really appreciated the assistance they were providing. They provided some airport analysis that the airport was finished. They provided medical capability. The State Department replaced it with its own medical capability. They provided communications capability. We replaced that with the State Department communications capability. And then they also provided direct security assistance personnel, wonderful colleagues from that unit. We were also, though, replacing them, as we do all over the world, by building an inherent State Department capability. And my colleagues believed we had achieved that right balance between what the State Department could provide and what the military had been providing to us when we were not ready to assume those responsibilities.

Mr. Connolly. Thank you. My time is up, Mr. Chairman.

Chairman Issa. The best part is you got that extra 30 seconds and some you wanted, very artfully.

Mr. Connolly. You are always generous. Thank you, Mr. Chairman.

Chairman Issa. With that, we go to the gentleman from Idaho, Mr. Labrador.

Mr. Labrador. Thank you, Mr. Chairman. One of the most difficult jobs I have as a Congressman is to call the families of the men and women who lose their lives in service of this country. And I take that responsibility very, very seriously.

I am looking right now--and I am really confused, Ambassador Kennedy, by some of the statements that your making today. In particular, the statement that has been addressed before. You said, for example: If any administration official, including any career official, were on television on Sunday, September 16, they would have said what Ambassador Rice said. The information she had at that point from the Intelligence Community--and I see how specific you are being--from the Intelligence Community, is the same that I had at that point.

Can you explain to me how it was that on September 12 you told congressional aides that you believed there was a terrorist attack?

Mr. Kennedy. Congressman, I told them that that was my personal opinion and that I also believed that it was, because of the nature of it and the lethality of it, that it was a complex attack.

Mr. Labrador. So how can you say here today that--the following day, you had an idea that it was a terrorist attack, in your opinion--I understand you claimed you are not a security expert--but in your opinion, it was a terrorist attack, how can you claim today that you would have made the same statements that Ambassador Rice would have made on TV?

Mr. Kennedy. Ambassador Rice was asked certain questions about information that she had in her possession. And that was the same information I had in my possession.

Mr. Labrador. But you came to a different conclusion from your information.

Mr. Kennedy. No, sir, I did not.

Mr. Labrador. Yes, you did. The statements are clear. Let me just ask you, you said today that there were multiple reports. And you didn't want to specify what those multiple reports were about what happened on September 11. Can you tell us at least when those multiple reports came out?

Mr. Kennedy. I would have to go back and refer to notes, sir.

Mr. Labrador. Did they come out a day after the incident, 2 days after the incident?

Mr. Kennedy. I will be glad to get that information.

Mr. Labrador. That is crucial. You knew you were coming here to testify before Congress. And you are coming here to tell us that there were multiple reports. You cannot tell us when those reports came out?

Mr. Kennedy. As I said earlier, Mr. Labrador, we were in an evolving series of reports over every day since the 12th of September.

Chairman Issa. Would the gentleman suspend?

Mr. Labrador. Yes.

Chairman Issa. Ambassador Kennedy, I want to make it clear, the gentleman's asking a reasonable question. To the best of your ability, approximating, we know that 7 days after the attack there were, in fact, false statements made. The gentleman's only trying to figure out how many reports continue to come to you 7 days, 6 days, 5 days, 4 days. Give us your best estimation and then we will let you be accurate for the record exactly.

The gentleman may continue.

Mr. Labrador. Can you answer that question?

Mr. Kennedy. Mr. Chairman, Mr. Labrador, I am not going to speculate on numbers that I don't have firmly in my head, sir.

Mr. Labrador. Can you tell me if there was at least one report before September 16 that contradicted what that Intelligence Community was telling you and Ambassador Rice? Can you answer that question?

Mr. Kennedy. I don't remember--I don't remember a report that contradicted what the Intelligence Community was telling us. No, sir, I do not remember.

Mr. Labrador. You just told us here there were several reports. And you said there were multiple reports that had different conclusions.

Mr. Kennedy. As I said in response to an earlier question, you are asking me to go into the nature of classified reports. And I cannot do that in this session.

Mr. Labrador. Okay. It is pretty clear that you are coming here with information about reports that you are unwilling to say. And I think we are going to have to have a classified hearing at some point.

I just have a quick question for Lieutenant Colonel Wood and Mr. Nordstrom. Given the information that you saw on TV and your knowledge of the situation in Libya, did you come to a conclusion as to whether this was a terrorist act or whether it was based on some film that was on the Internet? Lieutenant Colonel Wood.

Colonel Wood. It was instantly recognizable to me as a terrorist attack.

Mr. Labrador. Instantly recognizable.

Colonel Wood. Yes, sir.

Mr. Labrador. And why is that?

Colonel Wood. Mainly because of my prior knowledge there. I almost expected the attack to come. We were the last flag flying. It was a matter of time.

Mr. Labrador. Mr. Nordstrom, same question.

Mr. Nordstrom. The first impression that I had was that it was going to be something similar to one of the brigades that we saw there. Specifically, the brigade that has been named in the press that came to my mind was Ansar al-Sharia. It was a unit or a group that Lieutenant Colonel Woods' personnel and I had tracked for quite some time; we were concerned about. That specific group had been involved in a similar but obviously much smaller-scale incidents at the end of June involving the Tunisian consulate in Benghazi, where they stormed that facility and it was in protest to what they claimed was an anti-Islamic film in Tunis.

Mr. Labrador. Thank you very much. I just want to make it clear for the record that on September 16, Ambassador Rice went on TV. And I am assuming it was at the direction of this administration. She was not there on her own. I am sure she has better things to do on a Sunday morning. And she went to specifically tell the American people that all of the Intelligence information led to only one conclusion, when it is clear that Intelligence experts, security experts, and even Ambassador Kennedy, looking at the information that was happening on TV, could have concluded something different. I think that is outrageous and it is shameful.

Chairman Issa. I thank the gentleman. We now go to the gentleman from Illinois, who has been patiently waiting, Mr. Davis, for 5 minutes.

Mr. Davis. Thank you very much, Mr. Chairman. I want to thank all of the witnesses for participating by appearing here with us today. I also want to commend all of the brave men and women who risk their lives on a daily basis by serving in these high-risk areas. I also extend my condolences to the families of those who lost their lives or were injured during this tragic attack.

Following the death of longtime ruler Muammar Qadhafi, Libya and its citizens entered a critical transition period. Ambassador Stevens once described this period as ``a time of great excitement as the Libyan people first experienced freedom, but also a time of significant trepidation for what might come next." Ambassador Stevens, I think, obviously, was correct.

Ambassador Kennedy, Benghazi was the cradle of the revolution. Could you explain to us the importance of the diplomatic mission in Libya and the special post in Benghazi?

Mr. Kennedy. Thank you much, sir. Absolutely. Benghazi was the cradle of the revolution. There is essentially two major parts of Libya: east and west. In order to help the Libyans move forward, to help the Libyans take advantage of their newfound freedom and to build a democratic structure we all wish for any nation to have, we could not hunker down, we you could not stay out. As I mentioned earlier, the State Department has to go into harm's way. If we are going to advance U.S. national security interests, we cannot retreat.

We have to go, to use a colloquialism, we have to go where the action is. We will take every step we can to mitigate the risk to our personnel abroad. But we cannot end those risks, we cannot stay out of the action. We have to go there. And because, as you correctly posit, sir, because of the importance of Benghazi and the development of the new Libya, we had to have a forward operating location there and we had to have visits there by Ambassador Stevens.

Mr. Davis. Thank you very much. Mr. Nordstrom, on the other side of this, can you describe some of the challenges faced by security offices in analyzing security risks while allowing the diplomatic mission to interact with the local leaders and individuals in the population and still be effective?

Mr. Nordstrom. Absolutely. That was one of the tensions that we always had. We obviously understood the need to engage across a wide spectrum of programs. That was one of the main reasons we wanted that security resources, so that we could deploy sufficient resources to respond when there was a problem.

There was not open warfare at all times in Libya. Generally speaking, we saw a lot of improvements. It was fairly permissive during the daytime. Things started to heat up after hours. We had sort of a joke--I saw that it was in the newspaper--but we had a saying that in Libya, you would be fine until you are not.

Our problem was if someone found themselves in an issue. We had three officers specifically trapped in the prime minister's building when it was stormed by some fighters protesting a pay issue. Were we going to have sufficient people who could respond and navigate their way in and extricate those people? With time and with less resources, we were not going to have that.

One of the frustrating things that I found early on, and as I mentioned in my testimony, I was extremely pleased with the planning to get us into Libya. The frustrating thing that I found is once the first teams and the first TDYers started to expire at 60 days, there was a complete and total absence of planning that I saw in terms of what we were supposed to do from that point on. So when I requested resources, when I requested assets, instead of supporting those assets, I was criticized, and somehow it was my responsibility to come up with a plan on the ground and not the responsibility for DS. I raised that specific point in a meeting with the DS director in March; that 60 days, there was no plan. And it was hope that everything would get better.

Mr. Davis. Mr. Chairman, can I ask for unanimous consent for 15 additional seconds?

Chairman Issa. Without objection, so ordered.

Mr. Davis. Thank you very much. Ambassador, could you tell us how security risks at a post are evaluated and when are requests for increased staff or resources justified?

Mr. Kennedy. Yes, sir. We have a formula that we try to use. It is not a quadratic equation. But we look at the stability of the government, the threats against us, host government counterterrorism capability, the setback, the physical plant that we can muster, the ability to get sufficient local guard capability there. We put all that together. But in the end, this is an inherently risky operation. We cannot withdraw always to fortresses.

We look at this and then we try to place, as we believe we placed in Libya, on the basis of all the information we had to date, all the information we had, we put a security program into effect. That is what we call risk mitigation. We cannot end the risk. If we cannot achieve that level of risk mitigation, as we did in Damascus or as we have done in other locations, we simply remove our personnel from there because we cannot achieve that level of risk mitigation.

Mr. Davis. Thank you very much. I appreciate the courtesies.

Chairman Issa. Happy to do it. With that, as a favor to the former chairman of the full committee, I would ask unanimous consent he have 2 minutes to speak out of order. Without objection, so ordered.

Mr. Burton. Thank you very much, Mr. Chairman. I thank my colleagues. I will be real brief. First of all, Colonel Wood and Mr. Nordstrom, you said that al Qaeda is growing and it is even exceeding our goals in Libya right now. Is that correct?

Colonel Wood. Yes, sir, I make that assessment.

Mr. Burton. Mr. Nordstrom, you saw Ansar al-Sharia, which is another terrorist group loosely affiliated with al Qaeda, is very active there, too, and was involved?

Mr. Nordstrom. Interestingly, I would not say it was necessarily affiliated. It was actually one of the brigades which fell under the control, if you want to call it that, of the Libyan government.

Mr. Burton. But it is a terrorist organization as well?

Mr. Nordstrom. Not according to the Libyan government. It was actually one of their pseudo-militias.

Mr. Burton. What is your assessment?

Mr. Nordstrom. We were concerned that it was an extremist organization that wanted to bring----

Mr. Burton. Don't split words. It is a terrorist organization.

Okay. Ms. Lamb, there were three mobile security detachments; 18 people, six in each one of those detachments. They were supposedly asked to stay, the leadership did. And you were required to make a decision. They left and they were not replaced. They were supposed to be backfilled by diplomatic security agents. The 16 troops that--and you said you were watching in real-time, incidentally. That is very interesting. But the 16 troops that were supposed to be replaced, or were going to be requested to be replaced, you said no. And then you said they were going to be in Tripoli. But the fact of the matter is they not only worked in Tripoli, but when needed, they went down to Benghazi. Is that not right?

Ms. Lamb. I believe they made two to three trips.

Mr. Burton. I know, but they did go to Benghazi. And they could have gone to Benghazi. But they weren't there, so they were gone. And you decided that you thought that they shouldn't be redeployed.

Ms. Lamb. No, sir. As Under Secretary Kennedy has stated, the specialized skills that they brought when they came originally had been backfilled by other parts of the State Department. And the specialized skills----

Mr. Burton. But not with U.S. military?

Ms. Lamb. No, sir.

Mr. Burton. Okay. That is all I need to know. I really appreciate you folks taking all the time you have today.

Chairman Issa. I thank the gentleman. Colonel Wood, would you just respond? You looked like you were chomping at the bit when Ms. Lamb talked about specialized skills. She made an assessment. Would you agree with that?

Colonel Wood. No, sir, I would not agree. A special forces soldier is way above the skill level of a hired local national armed with a pistol, or even the MSD agents that were on the ground there as well.

Mr. Burton. Thank you.

Chairman Issa. Thank you. I think I remember the quote: Never take a knife to a gunfight.

With that, we go to the gentleman from Connecticut, Mr. Murphy.

Mr. Murphy. Thank you very much, Mr. Chairman. I add my gratitude to those members of the diplomatic corps and military who are putting their lives on the line for this country. And, of course, my sympathies to the families of those that were lost.

Mr. Chairman, I think you had maybe one of the most important lines of questioning about 20 minutes ago when you were inquiring as to what level of security might have really been necessary to repel this attack. I maybe wanted to pursue that one step further with you.

Chairman Issa. Would the gentleman yield for a second?

Mr. Murphy. Sure.

Chairman Issa. Your characterization is almost exact. I was actually talking about in order to extricate successfully those who otherwise died. Ultimately, I think it was made clear that you can't repel forever typically that size force.

Mr. Murphy. I simply wanted to expand on that line of questioning with Mr. Nordstrom. Because you very clearly do say in your testimony that the numbers that we are arguing about today, one or two additional unarmed security forces, six or seven armed security forces, may not have made the difference. You didn't really get the chance to answer that question fully, so I want to pose it again to you.

When you look back on this attack and you look at what was requested versus what would be necessary to either fully extricate everyone or to fully repel an attack such as this, do you think there is any amount of sort of reasonable numbers that could have been present on the ground there at the time that would have prevented this attack and this tragedy?

Mr. Nordstrom. Again, I am just hesitant to speculate on the specific numbers, but I think it goes without saying that having more resources on the ground is generally not something that you are going to turn down in a firefight. I would rather have more guns. I would rather have more Special Forces soldiers that have combat experience. And I would rather have more armed DS agents on the ground. Certainly the more of those you can bring to bear, I think the outcome is going to tip in your favor.

Mr. Murphy. And sort of a similar question to the ambassador. You know, we shudder at the notion that an attack like this could happen in the future, that this exceptional event in which 120 attackers, armed with assault rifles and rocket propelled grenades, could pose a threat to another installation. What is our position on trying to equip our outposts with the kind of armor and staffing that would be necessary to repel an attack of this size? Is that possible? And does this attack reframe your position and our country's position in terms of the resources that we give our outposts?

Mr. Kennedy. Sir, we are never going to be able to achieve a defense of an American facility abroad against that level of lethality with internally generated resources. What we try to do, and we have done it in many places around the world, and we are still constructing more and more, is we construct new embassies, and we build into those new embassies physical protections that we hope will permit our personnel who will have withdrawn into that building with the capability to wait until the host government, as they are required to do under the Vienna Convention and diplomatic law, responds to our attack.

But an attack of that kind of lethality, we are never going to have enough guns. We are a diplomatic service. We have I think some of the finest law enforcement professionals in the world in the diplomatic security Service, but we are not an armed camp ready to fight it out as the U.S. military does if there was an attack on a U.S. military facility in Afghanistan, using that as a current example.

Mr. Murphy. So let me just ask a variant of that question to you, Ambassador. What have we learned, and what has potentially changed? If we can't repel this kind of lethal attack, are there changes that you can share with us--some of them may be classified--as to how we protect our installations abroad?

Mr. Kennedy. The Accountability Review Board now, which is currently meeting, is going to judge whether our security there was adequate for the information that was available to us, whether we implemented it correctly, and whether or not there are lessons learned.

Mr. Murphy. So they will make recommendations?

Mr. Kennedy. They will make recommendations, yes, sir.

Mr. Murphy. Thank you very much.

Thank you, Mr. Chairman.

Chairman Issa. I thank the gentleman. The chair would announce that we know that there are some members who will have flights to catch since we are not in session broadly today. If anyone needs to go first, if you get close to your deadline, please inform the chair, and we will reserve the right to take people out of order.

But for now, we go to the gentleman from Pennsylvania, Mr. Meehan.

Mr. Meehan. Thank you, Mr. Chairman.

Mr. Nordstrom, you made a comment, a complete and total absence of planning.

Lieutenant Colonel Wood, you were brought in the first place to the country, part of a team that was in place to both be responsive, but to provide security, one of three teams of 16 people associated with the Department of Defense, not coming from the budget of Mrs. Lamb, but nonetheless providing. And I see a tale of two cities. That while you have that kind of force early on in the process, notwithstanding your requests, continuously that group is worked down from, three teams to finally one team towards the end, instead of 16, your final request in which it is eight.

At the same time, we see a worsening of the circumstances. I see this is a draft from Joan Polaschik in February of the month: Overall security conditions continue to be unpredictable. Large armed groups, not under the control of the central government. The continued presence of Security Support Teams was essential to provide static security in the absence of an appropriate local guard force.

Now, we saw with this a litany of issues, the IED thrown into the diplomatic post in Benghazi, the RPG attack on the Red Cross, the IED attack, a second one on the--we see a litany. Colonel Wood, was there the capacity to be able to provide the kind of security that you thought was necessary while things continued to get worse?

Colonel Wood. Yes, sir. I thought that was the genius behind the design and construct of the SST. It brought all the elements of government power together for the embassy, the diplomatic, the informational, military, and economic. It gave them the military side of that governmental power that we can project abroad. It gave them the expertise of some of the finest quality soldiers in the world and the backup resources that they could tap into at SOCAFRICA and AFRICOM as well to provide them with all the intelligence and additional capabilities. Why they would turn that asset down is best answered by themselves.

Mr. Meehan. Let me ask you about this process called normalization. There was an effort during this period of time as well to transition from people who were trained here by the United States, our soldiers, et cetera, who were in country, and to transition to trained locals, largely Libyans. As I understand it, there was a posting that would be put out where they just asked for people to apply for those positions. You were there. Part of your responsibility was to train those locals to be able to do the work. From your professional opinion, were there sufficient numbers sufficiently trained to be able to provide the kind of security that should have been necessary in the circumstances?

Colonel Wood. Sir, I think Eric Nordstrom can back me up on this. The individuals that were trained were local Libyans that we had hired. Indeed, you are correct that way. The SST participated with MSD in training some of those individuals. But the caliber and quality I think was subject. I can see where they are dealing with numbers on this end of the table, adding up numbers on a piece of paper. I think it reflects, from the description of the Benghazi compound, not being accurate in the fact that the RSO and security agents there had to sleep with their weapons. With the secure communications, they didn't have a complete understanding of how difficult it was or failed to recognize that.

Mr. Meehan. Ms. Lamb, why your response that this needs to be something in which these professionals need to be replaced by locals who, by a professional opinion, aren't sufficiently trained to do the work?

Ms. Lamb. Sir, this is the same model that we used in Sana'a. It has been very successful. These trained guards protected----

Mr. Meehan. Did you take any time to listen to the reports that were coming up during the period of time that the events were getting worse? Not the same model. But was there specific attention paid to the events in country?

Ms. Lamb. Yes. And at the same time, post had reduced their travel policy. Instead of moving with full motorcades, they were allowing personnel to go out with an embassy driver and a hard car. So the positions that were being filled by this team and by our team members had been reduced. They were using a quick reaction force that was available for multiple people to be moving with drivers. And it reduced the numbers that were needed at post.

When asked to do a function earlier in his testimony today, Eric Nordstrom cited the fact that he had requested 12 armed, plus six more. In essence, we had actually worked out with his desk officer, they had outlined a program that he needed 21 armed security personnel. We had made a commitment from Washington that we would provide him with 23. It has not dropped below that number since that commitment was made.

Mr. Meehan. Mr. Chairman, may I ask one just additional question not in response?

Chairman Issa. Briefly.

Mr. Meehan. Reports came.

Mr. Ambassador Kennedy, reports have been made, public reports, in which it has been stated that the imprisoned Omar Abdel-Rahman Brigades--this was on CNN--is believed to have possibly been one of the groups that is suspected of carrying out these terrorist attacks. CNN has reported that. Are you aware of any determinations at this point in time in which there has been any discussions within the State Department for the potential transfer or release of the blind sheik from American security?

Mr. Kennedy. I am unaware of any such discussion, sir.

Mr. Meehan. It says the State Department--this was in September--the State Department said that the topic had not come recently from any senior official in Egyptian authorities. So you are aware of no discussions whatsoever that involve the State Department for any kind of a transfer or release of the blind sheik from incarceration or otherwise?

Mr. Kennedy. That is correct, sir. I am unaware of any such discussion.

Mr. Meehan. Are you prepared on behalf of the State Department to make an unequivocal statement that there will not be a release of Abdel-Rahman.

Mr. Kennedy. I am not going to appear to avoid that question, sir, but I am the Under Secretary of State for Management. I have a series of responsibilities. And that is a question I will be glad to take for the record to get a complete State Department position for you.

Chairman Issa. I thank the gentleman.

Mr. Nordstrom, you were trying to answer the previous question. You want to respond on that.

Mr. Nordstrom. Yeah. I would like to actually, if I could, make a couple points on that. DAS Lamb mentioned that we had shifted to a, quote, lesser security profile. I would like to point out that that was done in March. That was done because we had 18 DS agents, and we were told that it was going to move to 12. Three MSD teams down to two MSD teams. There was an emergency action cable dated in March that specifically references that. And if I recall, in general recollection, that the tone of that was that since we had no choice, because we did not have the assets, we had no other option but to move to a model, not unlike in basketball, moving from man to man defense to a zone defense. So I think that is an important point to make.

The other point that was made earlier about the reduction of SST by six persons, that is something that Colonel Wood can back me up on as well. Those six SST did not leave country. Those six SST were still there on compound, could provide us internal defense support. What they were doing was involved in training and liaison with Libyan Special Forces.

Now, why were we doing that? Because as I have testified before, we had absolutely no ability to call upon a host nation force in the event that we were attacked. Our conclusion was the Libyan Special Forces was one such force that we might be able to count on. So we saw that very much as bolstering our internal defense and our footprint.

Chairman Issa. And Mr. Nordstrom, we placed in front of you something that a different whistleblower gave us. Is that the document you are referring to on May 28th? Or March 28th, I am sorry.

Mr. Nordstrom. This was the specific one in terms of a follow up for support. But there was an earlier document in March where we adjusted our movement transportation because we simply would not have the bodies to provide a security agent in each vehicle.

Chairman Issa. Thank you.

Ambassador Kennedy, I would now request that that earlier document that has been testified to be taken out of your in camera review and delivered to us. Would you do that?

Mr. Kennedy. I will take that request, sir. Yes, sir.

Chairman Issa. No, no, I am asking you now.

Mr. Kennedy. Mr. Chairman, I have not had--I have not had a chance to review the document. I have not had a chance to----

Chairman Issa. Wait, wait, wait. Wait a second. You can't come to a hearing and tell us that you haven't reviewed the documents you were going to allow in camera review of, and you have allowed it. Somebody on your staff has.

At this point, I will enter into the record the March 28, 2012, and specify that the earlier document is being withheld by the State Department. I regret that. Hopefully, you will reconsider so that it can be put in the record reasonably close to real time.

Mr. Kennedy. Mr. Chairman, if I might, I did not say I was denying it. I was simply saying that since I do not have the document in front of me, I have not had a chance----

Chairman Issa. David, would you put the document in front of the ambassador, please? You have it, don't you? It is in the in camera. Would you put it in front of the ambassador at least so he can at least see it in camera? You will have to remove it--it is an unclassified document--so that the ambassador can see it.

With that, would the staff please make sure--this one is being distributed while we will see whether we will get the other one.

Okay. It has been distributed.

Okay. Not wanting to delay this any further, we will come back to this, Ambassador.

With that, we go to the gentleman from Pennsylvania, Mr. Kelly, for 5 minutes. And I thank him for his patience.

Mr. Kelly. Thank you, Mr. Chairman.

And thank all of you for being here today.

The question really isn't about the patriotism and the heroics of the people that lost their lives that day. It's really, what can we do to prevent that from ever happening again? And I am kind of surprised. You know, I come from western Pennsylvania. And people look at things in maybe a little different fashion. When I am down here in Washington, D.C., amid all these brains and all the intelligence, and you get back home and you talk to people, if I were to say to you, Lieutenant Colonel Wood, what does 9/11 mean to you?

Colonel Wood. This last 9/11?

Mr. Kelly. No, just any--just 9/11. Like I would say December 7th. What does December 7th? 9/11----

Colonel Wood. It is an attack upon the United States of America.

Mr. Kelly. Mr. Nordstrom.

Mr. Nordstrom. The same.

Mr. Kelly. Ms. Lamb.

Ms. Lamb. The same.

Mr. Kelly. Ambassador.

Mr. Kennedy. Absolutely, sir.

Mr. Kelly. Okay. So if you can all connect the dots right here, why in the heck did it take so long for all these highly briefed and intelligent people to try and figure out that it actually wasn't a 15-minute YouTube video; it actually was a 9/11 event, a terrorist attack? Now, I don't know--look, this stuff about what is classified and not classified is getting confusing for me because I sat in a Members-only briefing.

And Mr. Chairman, I ask, this is on September the 20th with Secretary Clinton and some other personnel. Is that something we are allowed to talk about or not allowed to talk about?

Chairman Issa. If it was in a classified setting, the only thing that I would think would be appropriate is any inconsistencies you have seen in testimony today, you could relate. Otherwise, the specifics I couldn't judge it from the dais.

Mr. Kelly. Okay. Well, it comes down to this, what caused this?

And Ms. Lamb, I read through your testimony. I think it would be horrible to sit there and watch it in real time what was going on. And I read another account where, this is kind of strange, that same night, this is about the ambassador, at 8:30 p.m. the ambassador said good night to a visiting Turkish diplomat outside the compound, and the streets were empty. But at 9:40 p.m., noises, gunfire, and an explosion were heard by the agents located in the TOC and Building B.

It is absolutely preposterous to me that we would watch Ambassador Rice go out and say what happened 5 days later. That I would sit in a briefing, and it was, no, you have it all wrong. This is not a terrorist attack. This is a result of a 15-minute YouTube. Now, we are either in denial or unfortunately--and I don't if some of the Members are concerned, because I got to tell you; it is very unfortunate that terrorists don't recognize that this is an election year. And they tend to just do what they want any time they want to us. And when we have a weakened position around the world, and when we leave our embassies and our consulates and our people as unprotected as we do, and then we say, you know what, this is terrible because this is 27 days before an election, why are we bringing it up now?

And I ask the same question. Where the heck were we before 9/11, this 9/11? Why weren't we questioning it then? My goodness, 230 security instances in Libya between June of 2011 and July of 2012. Of those attacks, 48 took place in Benghazi, two of which at the U.S. diplomatic compound and the scene of the September 11th, 2012, terrorist attacks. And we are still saying I think it is the result of a video that was on YouTube. And this is based on intelligence.

Now, listen, I got to ask you, Ambassador Kennedy, because you say you couldn't possibly have had a different idea about it than

Secretary Rice did when she went before the Nation on September the 16th.

I am going to tell you this thing smells from every single end. Listen, it waddles like a duck and quacks like a duck; it is a duck. And for you to come in here and say, well, it was based on some of the things I knew, but I can't tell you all that I knew, we have got four Americans dead. And I got to tell you, it is very upsetting for me to go back home and look at those people in the eye, people who don't do what we do here, with all the briefings and all the intelligence, just guys that go out and work every day and women that go out and work every day, and they can come home, and they can figure it out. But we are still trying to figure it out and piece it together, and you watched it in real time? And the account wasn't there of the ambassador that night saying goodbye to a Turkish friend outside the gates and everything was quiet. But my goodness, those terrorists got ahold of--these Islamic extremists got ahold of that video, and between 8:30 and 9:40, they decided to just go crazy. And Africa is on fire.

And Mr. Nordstrom, thank you for pointing out, as Mr. Romney did, that hope is not a strategy.

And I feel sorry for you and Lieutenant Colonel Wood to have to come here because it is you who were on the ground. You are not watching it in some far away room in real time. Your people are there in real time. We have watched our colleagues be killed. And the question doesn't become, what is it that we didn't know? It is because we have become lax. We have dumbed down. We have turned down the dial.

You know, by the way, at the same time--and I know it is about the money to some degree, right? Although I saw a whole list of all the things that we were able to do. Apparently, it wasn't for the money there. You know that the embassy in Vienna in early May, we did a beautiful, beautiful presentation of the embassy going green. Spent $110,000 on a little electrical thing to plug the cars in. Had two Volts there. Had 100 people there. We are sipping champagne and eating hors d'oeuvres, and my goodness, my goodness. On September 11th, we had a tough day. And a couple of bumps in the road.

Chairman Issa. I thank the gentleman.

Mr. Kelly. I got to say, Mr. Chairman, I appreciate it. I know I am going over. But the people of America should be outraged to have to sit here and listen to what we are saying and say, what are we doing to protect the other embassies and our personnel? They are true patriots. But you know what they rely on? The State Department for their security. And we let them down.

Chairman Issa. Thank you, Mr. Kelly.

Mr. Kennedy. Mr. Chairman?

Chairman Issa. There was no question there, Ambassador. I perceive no question. The gentlemen felt he had no question.

With that, we go to the gentleman from Florida for 5 minutes, Mr. Ross.

Mr. Ross. Thank you, Mr. Chairman.

Thank you. Mr. Nordstrom, earlier in your testimony you were discussing your recollection of a conversation that you had had with two agents in the room regarding the denial of the extension of the SST. Now, and it was your understanding that you were not to request an extension at that point. Is that correct?

Mr. Nordstrom. That is correct.

Mr. Ross. And who was on the other end of the line that told you that?

Mr. Ross. I was on the telephone call with DAS Lamb.

Mr. Ross. Was Ms. Lamb on the phone call with you?

Mr. Nordstrom. That is. I am sorry.

Mr. Ross. So she did tell you that?

Mr. Nordstrom. That is correct.

Mr. Ross. Okay. Now, she, just the other day in an interview with the committee, indicated that on your July 9 cable to Washington requesting security personnel, you didn't formally request an SST extension. In fact, you just made a recommendation. Can you explain if there is a difference between a recommendation and a request?

Mr. Nordstrom. I in post felt that was a pretty clear request for resources.

Mr. Ross. Had you done it before with the idea that it was a request?

Mr. Nordstrom. I believe it was also titled ``request for continued TDY staffing."

Mr. Ross. And it was a denial of that extension.

Mr. Nordstrom. Well, actually, we never actually received a response.

Mr. Ross. Other than that phone conference that you were on.

Mr. Nordstrom. Correct. We never received a response----

Mr. Ross. And as a result of that phone conference where you were denied, did you seek any further effort to follow up or make a re-request?

Mr. Nordstrom. I believe actually to clarify, the telephone call was prior to sending in the cable. What we decided, since we continued to get resistance, instead of specifically asking for SST, or MSD, or whatever, we just said, you know what, give us the 13 bodies, wherever you come from, and that's the way in which we crafted the cable.

Mr. Ross. Now, Mrs. Lamb, you testified in an interview with this committee that you trusted your RSOs in the field, such as Mr. Nordstrom. Now, how do you square that statement with you telling Mr. Nordstrom that you would not support an extension of the SST?

Ms. Lamb. The cable that he sent in indicated that any of the categories----

Mr. Ross. But before the cable was the phone conversation.

Ms. Lamb. That is correct.

Mr. Ross. But you wouldn't support his request or his recommendation at that time.

Ms. Lamb. Because we had Department of State diplomatic security assets that could do the same functions of the remaining----

Mr. Ross. And that was explained to him as well?

Ms. Lamb. Yes, sir.

Mr. Ross. Now, Lieutenant Colonel Wood, I understand that you were the senior officer of the SST team. Is that correct?

Colonel Wood. That is correct, sir.

Mr. Ross. And do you have any reason to believe that if you had to go up your chain of command at AFRICOM for a request from the State Department that they extend the tour of duty of an SST that your chain of command would not grant that?

Mr. Wood. General Ham was fully supportive of extending the SST as long as they felt they needed them.

Mr. Ross. So the resources were available for the SST.

Colonel Wood. Absolutely.

Mr. Ross. And had they been there, they would have made a difference, would they not?

Colonel Wood. They made a difference every day they were there when I was there, sir. They were a deterrent effect.

Mr. Ross. Thank you. Now, Ambassador Kennedy, just real quickly, and everybody has been beating this, and I understand it, but I just want to reconcile it in my own mind. Here we have got the official statement of the State Department that this protest, this attack, was all as a result of a video that was controversial. But yet the next day, the President of Libya comes out and says, well, it was not as a result of a controversial video. In fact, he had no doubt that it was an act of terrorism. And so I guess my question is, is it that the

Libyan intelligence is so superior to the American intelligence that they knew within 24 hours that it was a terrorist attack, and within 6 days, we are still saying it was a result of a video?

Mr. Kennedy. Mr. Ross, I am going to take a liberty here, and I am going to correct one point, if I might. You asked the colonel, would his team have made a difference?

Mr. Ross. No, sir, you are on my time right here, so I have to control this.

Mr. Kennedy. His team was not----

Chairman Issa. The gentleman from Florida controls the time for questions he wishes to ask.

Mr. Kennedy. Very good, sir.

Mr. Ross. So the intelligence between the Libyans and the Americans just wasn't the same. Apparently, they were more superior. Now, if they were more superior in their intelligence, and you testified just earlier that you were still gathering information, that is why you didn't say it was officially a terrorist attack, then why in the world did you say it was anything at all when you put Jay Carney out there and Ambassador Rice to say that this is a result of an inflammatory reaction to a controversial film?

Sir, it begs the question. What happened was it was a result of political pressure trumping professional protocol, was it not?

Mr. Kennedy. Mr. Ross, I have been a career Foreign Service officer for 39 years. I have served every President since Richard Nixon. I have directly served six Secretaries of State, Democratic and Republican. On my honor, no, none, political pressure was applied to me in this case by anyone at the State Department, at the National Security Council, or at the White House.

Mr. Ross. Then it was a professional protocol malpractice.

I yield back.

Chairman Issa. I thank the gentleman.

We now go to the gentleman from South Carolina, Mr. Gowdy.

Mr. Gowdy. Thank you, Mr. Chairman.

Mr. Chairman, for almost a year there was an escalating pattern of violence directed towards the United States and other Western targets in Libya: Attacks on the consulate in Benghazi; attacks and assassination attempts on the British ambassador; attacks on the International Red Cross; attacks on courthouses; judges assassinated; culminating on September the 11th in the murder of four Americans, including our ambassador to Libya.

Before those four murders, Mr. Chairman, just a few weeks before that, our embassy in Libya said this to the Department of State: The security condition in Libya remains unpredictable, volatile, and violent.

So Mr. Chairman, despite what would appear to any reasonably objective observer as an escalating pattern of violence, including sophistication, coordination, and management, this administration blamed the murder of our ambassador and three others on a video.

Don't take my word for it, Mr. Chairman, let's look at what Ambassador Rice herself said: Our current assessment is that what happened in Benghazi was, quote, in fact initially a spontaneous reaction. I don't know what the phrase ``in fact'' means in diplomatic legalese. I can tell you what it means in a courtroom, Mr. Chairman. It means it is a fact. And she went on national television, and she said, not as this ambassador has said, that I am not going to speculate, that I have got to get all the information; she said, in fact, this was a spontaneous reaction to what had just transpired hours before in Cairo, almost a copycat of the demonstrations against our facility in Cairo, which were prompted, of course, Mr. Chairman, by a video is what she said.

And then she proceeds to say the attack was spontaneous. I can think of few things, Mr. Chairman, more antithetical to spontaneity than a 12-month long prologue of violence in Libya.

And then she said she relied solely and squarely on the information the intelligence community provided. Mr. Chairman, I would like to have another hearing where we can ask Ambassador Rice under oath, who told you what when? You are going to blame the intelligence community; you come before this committee and you tell us who told you it was a video. Who in the intelligence community said it? Who in the diplomatic community blamed this on a video?

And then we move to Jay Carney, who is the spokesperson for the leader of the free world. This is what he said, Mr. Chairman: ``I am saying based on information that we--our initial information that includes all information--we saw no evidence to back up claims by others that this was a preplanned or premeditated attack. What we saw was evidence that it was sparked by the reaction to this video. And that is what we know thus far based on evidence, concrete evidence''.

Mr. Chairman, you know that in a former life, I spent a little time in the courtroom. So when I hear the phrase ``concrete evidence,'' it means something to me. That is even stronger language than simply saying something is in fact. So two representatives of this administration gave demonstrably false statements, not just to us, but to our fellow citizens on national television. Now, is the explanation for those demonstrably false statements, as my colleague from Florida just asked, was it negligence? Was it just a reckless disregard for the truth? Or was it more nefarious than that?

Mr. Chairman, the American people are reasonable. People understand investigations take time. People don't expect you to speculate until you have all the facts. What they will not forgive, Mr. Chairman, is being misled. We want our questions answered. And I want them answered by the people that went out before the American people and sought to mislead them by blaming this on a video when there is no evidence, concrete or otherwise, to support the assertions made by this administration.

Mr. Chairman, I just had a conversation with Jason Chaffetz out back. And I hope he doesn't mind me saying this. He still gets emotional talking about what he saw in Libya. There were four brave Americans who died under circumstances that we can scarcely fathom, the terror, the fear, the anarchy of being killed in that fashion. They did what their country asked them to do. They stood post under dangerous circumstances even after requests for security were denied. They stood their post. The least we can do is stand this meager post that we have been assigned and demand that this administration speak the truth to the people it is supposed to serve. This was never about a video. It was never spontaneous. This is terror. And I want to know why we were lied to. And I yield back.

Mr. Cummings. Mr. Chairman?

Chairman Issa. The ranking member.

Mr. Cummings. I have to, as an officer of the court, I have to--I am looking at the transcript from the date, and I will read it, if you want. I mean, to sit here and accuse one of our fellow citizens and Secretary Rice of lying, that is a very, very serious statement. And I am very concerned about that because I mean, she made it clear over and over again that she was dealing with the information that she had at that moment. And she said it over--I looked at every single interview. I think we have to be very careful. Just as the gentleman talks about he wants some truth and all that to come forward, I would be happy to join and have Ms. Rice come up here.

But I think we have got to be careful, a distinguished attorney, a distinguished woman, and she made it emphatic, she said this is the information I have at this moment.

Chairman Issa. I appreciate the gentleman's comment.

I would inform the committee that the ranking member and I will be requesting a classified interview at the earliest possible date, perhaps as early as next week, that would be similar to the one that Ambassador Kennedy was in yesterday. And we will inform both sides as soon as that has been granted.

Additionally, it is our intention to follow all of the clues to where they lead, including how a week after this, people could still say with certainty that in fact something was true that we now know not to be true.

And I appreciate the ranking member's statement. And I thank the gentleman from South Carolina.

With that, we now go to the ever patient senior member of the--I am sorry. We now go to the equally patient gentleman from Texas, Mr. Farenthold.

Mr. Farenthold. I am not sure my wife would agree with you on patience.

Chairman Issa. She is actually more patient than you. We have met her.

Mr. Farenthold. Anyway, after listening to Mr. Gowdy, you know, we have a list of four brave Americans who gave their life for this country, Ambassador Stevens, Sean Smith, Glen Doherty, and Tyrone Woods.

And I think Mr. Gowdy hit it on the head, at best, this is negligence. We have an ongoing pattern of requests for more help and it not going up the chain of command. How many more people are we going to have to add to this list? And that is what I want to pursue in this line of questioning.

And I will start with Mrs. Lamb and Ambassador Kennedy. Are there other embassies similarly situated, other State Department outposts that are asking for more help because of volatile situations that are not getting it?

Ms. Lamb. In volatile locations, no, sir.

RSOs just need to confer with their post management, because it is a matter of bed space and logistical issues and the requests and the justification for what these personnel will do, and it is granted. If we don't have permanent assignments to put there, we immediately put temporarily assigned agents there.

Mr. Farenthold. So there is not a budget problem; it is not you all don't have the money to do this?

Ms. Lamb. Sir, if it is a volatile situation, we will move assets to cover that.

Mr. Farenthold. Would you have considered--at the time, did you consider Libya to be a volatile situation?

Ms. Lamb. Sir, absolutely. And the desk officer sat--talked and sent emails and came to an agreement with Eric Nordstrom. We were trying to get a clearly defined list of exactly what he needed out there.

Mr. Farenthold. So how long does this have to get tied up in bureaucratic red tape? To me, it is like saying we are on fire, let's figure out how many firemen to send. Let's just send some.

Ms. Lamb. Sir, we did provide everything that he asked for.

Mr. Kennedy. Sir, do you want my response to that, too?

Mr. Farenthold. Yes, please.

Mr. Kennedy. Thank you very much, sir.

The answer is we did provide resources. And as a point of clarification following on your question, there has been a large discussion here about the SST team headed by Colonel Wood. The SST team was the Tripoli team.

Mr. Farenthold. Okay. I want to go to Mr. Nordstrom, because he was there on the field. You guys, I was talking to you guys about what was happening in D.C.

Do you think it was on fire, and you needed more people and you communicated that urgently up the chain of command?

Mr. Nordstrom. I think that my cables stand as they are in terms of addressing the assertion from DAS Lamb that there wasn't a specific or detailed list.

For the members that are here, they can see that this is more than detailed. I also have a number of memorandums that went back as far as February detailing not just the numbers we needed but the specific hours those people would be working and the duties.

Mr. Farenthold. And you didn't get them.

Mr. Nordstrom. I think the question to be asked is, again, as was asserted after my July 9th cable, that the plan was to source our security needs from the Department of State rather than from the

Department of Defense. I think the question is, were those resources ever provided? And I think the answer is no.

Mr. Farenthold. Okay. You have anything to add, Lieutenant Colonel Wood?

Colonel Wood. No.

Mr. Farenthold. Okay. I realize you guys don't, Lieutenant Colonel Wood and Mr. Nordstrom, you all don't have the level of information that Ms. Lamb and Ambassador Kennedy have. But having been in the biz, so to speak, do you think there are other embassies out there and other State Department facilities similarly situated to what we had in Libya that are at risk today?

Colonel Wood. Sir, it is my impression that a cookie-cutter approach or some sort of a plan was being applied to us. That is what we felt down there in the field as we tried to work this situation. And certainly Libya met none of those requirements.

Mr. Farenthold. Yeah. As a former military person, historically, it is been the Marines that have protected our embassy and for a variety of political situations. And I need point no further than Iraq, with the huge amount of money we are spending to protect our embassy with contractors, when for political reasons or whatever we are not putting Marines in. Do you think that is a good idea that we are doing that, we are not relying on the Marines?

Colonel Wood. Sir, I think there is definitely a place for it. It needs to be studied. And I think each location is going to present you with a different situation that needs to be looked at for the merits on its own merits.

Mr. Farenthold. And I think as we have the Arab Spring coming, and we have the freedom and democracy coming to these Arab states, we have got to be aware that sometimes there are going to be times of transition when countries are not stable. There may be election results that we don't like or when people who don't like us are elected. And I think we need to take this as a lesson that we need to be much more proactive and project more strength so this doesn't happen in times that can change literally in a matter of hours. I see I am out of time, so I will yield back.

Chairman Issa. I thank the gentleman.

With that, we are going to go to our very patient invited Members of Congress, starting with the senior member of the Foreign Affairs Committee, Mr. Rohrabacher.

Mr. Rohrabacher. Thank you very much, Mr. Chairman.

And as chairman of the Oversight and Investigations Subcommittee of Foreign Affairs, I appreciate you taking the lead in making sure that we are deeply getting in deep into an issue that is important to the American people.

It has been suggested that budget cuts were responsible for a lack of security in Benghazi. I would like to ask, Ms. Lamb, you made this decision personally; was there any budget consideration and lack of budget which led you not to increase the number of people in the security force there?

Ms. Lamb. No, sir. And it----

Mr. Rohrabacher. Okay. That is all I need. Thank you very much.

Okay. So it wasn't a lack of money, as we have heard by some people trying to suggest that. Was it a lack of intelligence? Was this a failure of intelligence? Or was it a lack of competence? Or is this just something that will happen? No matter how we try or how competent we are, we are going to lose lives like this.

Ms. Lamb. Sir, this was an unprecedented attack in size and ferocity, as the words of RSO Eric Nordstrom. And as long as we have the need to be outside of the wire in these volatile countries, we can't defend against that.

Mr. Rohrabacher. Okay. Let me just note that I do not believe that that is the case. But I think that you honestly believe that.

. There are other factors involved here that make us vulnerable or not vulnerable to these type of evil forces that are in the world. So I would like to--I know we have touched on these issues of preparedness, et cetera, and the bureaucratic things that people go through to make sure that we don't have this type of suffering and loss of life. But I would like to focus on not the bureaucratic planning and what could have been done and not done; I would like to focus on one other area. We heard from one of our colleagues a list of names of those killed during the Reagan administration who were killed by terrorists. I worked in the Reagan administration. I can tell you not once, when all of these Americans were being killed by terrorists, did the administration in any way try to excuse or in any way these murderous attacks as some sort of spontaneous outrage due to something that the administration had done or an American citizen had done. Big difference. We are talking about a mindset that may encourage evil forces in the world to kill Americans.

This administration has been bowing and scraping to try to prove its sincerity and friendship seeking to the Islamic world since day one. It has projected not strength, but weakness and has demoralized our friends and emboldened our enemies, which perhaps had something to do with people who took a long time to plan out this kind of attack. This mindset might be seen in a psychological minimizing of the threat of radical Islam in general and maybe even specific situations. This mindset might also be seen in situations like this when we are trying to describe and come to the realization of what happened in a horrific terrorist attack on our people.

For example, there is a mindset that might lead people who are here testifying not even to use the word terrorism in their testimony when we are talking about a terrorist attack that murdered our ambassador. That is not your fault. But there is a mindset there somewhere that says those--the word terrorism doesn't come into your written testimony. I would also suggest that we need to--that mindset may be when people jump to the conclusion, because it is an easy conclusion, to blame a film maker and let terrorists off the hook for responsibility of these terrorist acts. That mindset of minimizing the threat of terrorism and blaming it on us, freedom of speech in America, we permitted a film that created outrage overseas, instead of putting the blame where it belongs.

And that is where the testimony from Mr. Kennedy comes in. Mr. Kennedy, we need to understand that whole scenario after this event to understand the mindset that may be at play here. We need to understand the scenario of what happened. Six days afterwards, we know the American people were given false information about who was responsible. You were here today, and you are unable to give us a view of how that came about. And the fact is, as far as this Member of Congress is concerned, you were engaged in stonewalling or a coverup or whatever it is. Lets me ask you it flat out. Did anyone tell you not to answer this question?

Mr. Kennedy. Absolutely no one.

Mr. Rohrabacher. So you have taken it upon yourself not to answer what is a simple scenario. When did you first know about this? Or as they said during the Nixon years, when did you know? What did you know? And when did you know about it? But you are not able to give us that answer.

Mr. Kennedy. If I could respond, sir?

Chairman Issa. The gentleman's time has expired, but the ambassador may respond.

Mr. Kennedy. Let me quote exactly what Susan Rice said on that Sunday talk show: ``But our current assessment, based on the information that we have at present, is that in fact what this began as was spontaneous, not premeditated."

Mr. Rohrabacher. Right.

Mr. Kennedy. She said very specifically, ``based on our current assessment."

Mr. Rohrabacher. And Mr. Chairman, the retort to that is we are not just talking about her one statement. If you notice, this innuendo and this blame for the time immediately after was what we heard--all heard about it. It was the film. How many times? The Secretary of State used the word the film. So it is not just one speech that you are talking about, which may or may not be correct. This is something that we need to get to the heart of the matter.

Thank you, Mr. Chairman.

Chairman Issa. I thank the gentleman.

We now go to the gentlelady from Florida, who is extremely familiar with law enforcement and how it is to be worked, Ms. Adams.

Mrs. Adams. Thank you, Mr. Chairman.

And thank the committee for allowing me to sit here today.

Ms. Lamb, I am a former law enforcement officer, as I know you have stated you are. So I am going to go along that line, as my colleague who is a prosecutor. We tend to listen very intently and are trained to do so. So I believe you will understand some of the questions I am going to ask you. And yes or no is fairly easy on some of them, like Mr. Burton asked you, was it your sole discretion to deny the extra manpower. Yes or no? Your sole discretion. Was it your sole discretion to deny the request from Mr. Nordstrom?

Ms. Lamb. No.

Mrs. Adams. Who above you had to approve that?

Ms. Lamb. The response cable would be approved by two senior---

-

Mrs. Adams. And who are they?

Ms. Lamb. The director of diplomatic security and the Assistant Secretary.

Mrs. Adams. Names, please?

Mr. Lamb. Scott Bultrowicz and Eric Boswell.

Mrs. Adams. Thank you.

Now, as a former law enforcement officer, I recognize there are certain dates that law enforcement across our great Nation prepare for because we believe they are significant to certain groups, one of which is September 11th. And it is significant to which group, Ms. Lamb? Which group would make that significant?

Ms. Lamb. I am not sure I am following you.

Mrs. Adams. Which terrorist group finds September 11th significant?

Ms. Lamb. I am sure all terrorist groups find it.

Mrs. Adams. But mostly al Qaeda, would you not agree? Yes or no. If you don't agree, then say you don't agree.

Ms. Lamb. Yes, I am sure.

Mrs. Adams. Thank you. So, we have requests, over 230 clear incidents, we have, you know, bombings that have already entered our compound. Yet multiple requests, over 230 clear incidents, violence erupting everywhere around, and you and your agency deny the security personnel that they have requested. And then, on September 11th, which is known to be one of those dates that all of law enforcement and many people around the world look at--and I hope you helped her out, Mr. Ambassador, I am watching very closely and intently, as I was earlier--why is it that after all of that, that we have our ambassador to the U.N. go to the talk shows on the Sunday afterwards and many other people from your agency, even here today, that say, well, with the information that we had, why is it that they said it was a film, when everything, all my law enforcement training taught me, that it was pointing quite differently? Can you ask me--answer me did you believe, you, on September 11th and the morning after, did you believe that it was a video and not a terrorist attack? Yes or----

Ms. Lamb. With 35 years of experience, I choose to wait until the investigation is complete before drawing a conclusion.

Mrs. Adams. Well, that is good. Because that is the other thing I wanted to ask about, too. With my investigation experience, I also know that you follow the leads very carefully, and you don't go out and immediately claim one thing until you do have the facts, Mr. Ambassador.

So, on September 14th, Ms. Nuland from your agency said that we have an open FBI investigation on the death of these four Americans. We are not going to be in a position to talk at all about the U.S.

Government may or may not be learning about how any of this happened, not who they were, not how they happened, not what happened to Ambassador Stevens, not any of it until, Justice Department is ready to talk about the investigation. So you did talk about it yesterday. So did the Department of Justice say that they are ready to talk about it and you, therefore, can go ahead and give up that information?

Mr. Kennedy. What we talked about yesterday----

Mrs. Adams. I am asking Ms. Lamb.

Ms. Lamb. I am sorry, I thought you were speaking with Ambassador Kennedy.

Mrs. Adams. Did Department of Justice say, okay, our investigation is at a point you can now release this information? Yes or no?

Ms. Lamb. No.

Mrs. Adams. So you went ahead, and on September 14th, 3 days after the attack, said you wouldn't release it, and then yesterday, you did release it, but the Department of Justice did not----

Ms. Lamb. The FBI has cleared everything that we have said here today.

Mrs. Adams. And yesterday also.

Ms. Lamb. I was not in the briefing yesterday.

Mrs. Adams. Mr. Ambassador, yesterday also?

Mr. Kennedy. The material we used yesterday was drawn from the same pool that the FBI cleared.

Mrs. Adams. The Department of Justice said, it is okay to release that information.

Mr. Kennedy. We presented, we presented in a closed session to the Congress.

Chairman Issa. Is the gentlelady referring to the press avail?

Mrs. Adams. I am.

Chairman Issa. It is your press conference in which you sort of stated a lot of things categorically for I guess everybody except Fox.

Mr. Kennedy. I think the distinction--I think the distinction I would draw, Congresswoman, is that there is a difference between the investigation to determine who the perpetrators were and a rendition of the facts that we now know ran out. So there is a timeline, and then there is the cause. And that is the distinction I humbly am making.

Mrs. Adams. But your spokesperson said you would not--who they are, who they were, not how they happened, not what happened to the ambassador, not any of it until Justice Department is ready to talk. Is the Justice Department ready to talk on this?

Mr. Kennedy. The Justice Department is certainly not ready to talk about the first two of the----

Chairman Issa. The gentlelady's time is expired.

And I don't think you are going to get an answer out of the gentleman on that subject. I appreciate your effort.

The chair would inform everyone that we are not terribly interested in a second round. I am going to ask a couple of quick, very quick clarifying questions, and then if anyone really has a burning desire, they may. Otherwise, we will conclude.

Everyone has been very generous with their time.

And it really boils down to there was a statement that hasn't been covered any further, Ambassador Kennedy, that the DC-3, an aircraft that was available, was taken away because, quote, commercial airline capacity was created. Correct?

Mr. Kennedy. Correct.

Chairman Issa. Okay. So why are there five fixed-wing aircraft, at least one of them very big, quite a few of them big, and 35 helicopters in Iraq, even though they have commercial aircraft?

Mr. Kennedy. There is no safe commercial air service available within Iraq. There is safe commercial air service available to and from Libya, sir.

Chairman Issa. Okay. So Libya is safe; Iraq isn't.

Mr. Kennedy. In terms of air service, specifically to move people in and out of the country.

Chairman Issa. Okay. I just want to make it clear. Additionally, and I am not trying to unreasonably use a prop, but I was given it, and I used it in an earlier hearing, everyone that goes to Iraq gets one of these, or at least an opportunity. This is from a brigade-size force of diplomatic security personnel.

Thank you.

I guess it looks better this way.

Do you recognize--have any of you even it in Iraq, Ambassador? Ms. Lamb?

Mr. Kennedy. I have never seen that, sir.

Chairman Issa. It has been told to us in testimony that between 80 and 100 diplomatic security personnel have been working Iraq over the last year. Is that roughly right?

Ms. Lamb. Eighty-eight, yes, sir.

Chairman Issa. Okay. So Iraq, a place that the war is supposed to be over, it is safe, has like 6,000 contract personnel, 14,000 of our government employees direct and indirect, and 80 DSS, but you couldn't spare six more for Libya. Is that correct?

Ms. Lamb. Sir----

Chairman Issa. Or you didn't see the need for them.

Ms. Lamb. No, sir, I am not sure where the number six is coming from.

Chairman Issa. That was the difference between two crews and three crews. It would have been a difference of similar numbers had you backfilled with military personnel that were available and offered to you by General Ham.

Ms. Lamb. Okay. Sir, as I said, Eric Nordstrom and the desk officer agreed on a number. We fulfilled that number. If he needed six additional people----

Chairman Issa. Okay.

Mr. Nordstrom, you are saying you don't agree on the number. That is probably the most important thing to get here straight. The number available on September 11th is not consistent with what you thought was the need when you were last in country. Is that correct?

Mr. Nordstrom. Whether or not the numbers were agreed upon, when I left, we did not have the 12 numbers that were quote-unquote agreed upon.

Chairman Issa. Thank you very much.

I want to thank all of the witnesses. Okay. Then I won't close at this point. I recognize the ranking member.

Mr. Cummings. Just a few questions.

Just following up on what the chairman just talked about, Ambassador, what is the budget for Iraq's embassy? Just an estimation.

Mr. Kennedy. I think the budget is probably up close to a $700 million, $800 million run rate.

Mr. Cummings. What about Libya?

Mr. Kennedy. Much smaller than that, sir. I didn't bring that exact number with me.

Mr. Cummings. Ms. Lamb, you have been--I listened to the description that you gave of what happened. And somebody asked the question a moment ago, basically, why you made the decisions that you did make. And I got to ask you, I am assuming that you were always concerned about the safety of the folks that were there. Is that right?

Ms. Lamb. Absolutely.

Mr. Cummings. And you, I assume you used your best judgment trying to make those decisions?

Ms. Lamb. Absolutely. In fact, we sent an email to post right before the last MSD team left, offering to leave them there to continue training even though they didn't have the full complement for another class of armed bodyguards. And basically, we gave post two options. If they needed them, they could keep them there. We would be happy to train a lesser class. And then we also gave the option that we could come back a month later and train a full class. And post chose to allow the MSD team to leave and come back at a later date. And these are assets that would have been on the ground there as well.

Mr. Cummings. The reason why I am asking you these questions is because I am just trying to put myself in your place right now. And the implications that you are either incompetent, that you didn't give a damn, or you are some kind of Scrooge, and I don't think you are any of those. And I just want you to just, you know, just give you an opportunity to respond to that.

Ms. Lamb. Sir, we do have limited resources, and it is very important that we have our regional security officers in coordination with their emergency action committees at post and with their ambassadors clearly lay out and articulate exactly what they need and why they need it. And Eric Nordstrom did a fantastic job. He had a very difficult job as the first RSO going in there. And sometimes putting pen to paper and sitting down and coordinating a transition exit strategy, especially for the SST was very difficult. And we engaged him on a regular basis to try to come up with this exit strategy that we could all agree upon and to move into it gradually.

Every time a mobile security division left, there were three, before each team left, they spoke with RSO Nordstrom, and they spoke with the Ambassador at post and they reviewed everything that they had accomplished and what the post needs still going forward and they got permission to leave before they left post.

Mr. Cummings. Are you satisfied with your decisions?

Ms. Lamb. I made the best decisions I could with the information I had, sir.

Mr. Cummings. Thank you very much.

Chairman Issa. Thank you.

Mr. Kelly, you wanted to make a brief statement in closing?

Mr. Kelly. I do, Mr. Chairman. Thank you, and all of you thanks for being here.

I know there's incredible pressure put on you but you are all at part of the executive branch, not so much the two officers, and there is a time, and I said earlier, these things come at a bad time and people talk about being 27 days before the election but every once in a while you have to worry more about running the country than running for reelection, and you have to make decisions as the executive, and you have to make sure that the staff you have on board is really somebody that you can rely on all the time.

These folks have to rely on you to make the decisions. While we can do some things in appropriations and oversight, it does come from the executive branch that all of these things fall into place. If you look at the organizational chart of this government, the State Department, Secretary of State has a great, great deal of responsibility. We lost four American lives. And I would think that as we go on, we have to ask these type of questions, and we have to ask what did we learn from the losses?

And if we do have people out there that are in harm's way, are we protecting them the way we should? Are we making the commitment to them that they made to us? They put their lives on the line. And then I keep hearing, well, we didn't have the resources. But that is not true. It is priorities that count. How do you prioritize those moneys that you have?

And I have got to tell you. I have watched this thing now since September 11. I am trying to understand why in the world we've sat back and we continue to try to find out who to blame. The blame is that there is a group of people in the world that are really bad people, but we have to be able to deal with them. But other question is we put our people in harm's way. Did we do the best job we could to protect them? They put their lives on the line. Did we do everything we could to protect them? And after what has happened in Benghazi what have we learned from that? And I know you are in law enforcement, I would tell the CSI Benghazi there is not a crime scene that has not been more contaminated than the one that is there right now. How would we learn from that after what we have allowed to have happen?

So I know that it has been a long day for all of us for you specifically, but for those four Americans and the families that lost those lives, it is a much longer day. And for those, Lieutenant Colonel Wood, Mr. Nordstrom, those are your colleagues. That hits you deeper than any of us, so I do appreciate your being here. I know how difficult it is. But I would like to say that as elected officials, we have a commitment to do, when we took our oath of office. It has nothing to do with Republicans or Democrats. It has to do now with Americans and patriotism. And we better start to be able to look at this and place emphasis on where it needs to be, and Mr. Chairman I thank you very much.

Chairman Issa. I thank you. Mr. Jordan.

Mr. Jordan. Thank you, Mr. Chairman, I will be brief here. In a 13-month time frame, we had 230 security instances in Libya. When the 231st happens, the administration blames it on a video. We got two guys on the ground who repeatedly asked for additional security personnel and are denied, denied by people who have never been to the country they have been in for months at a time. There is a process in place, according to Ambassador Kennedy's testimony and statements, where professionals come together and they make assessments and decisions about what the field is requesting.

Earlier, not in my questioning with you, Ambassador, you said factors that you look at, and I didn't get all of them listed, but three that I did jot down, stability of the government, threats against it and facility concerns. Well certainly in those three, there was nothing in Libya that would say they shouldn't get what they are asking for. The stability of this government, the government is a transitional government, that is the name of it. Threats against us, we had 230, facility concerns, you have admitted that in testimony the facility wasn't up to code.

So I guess I just want, it seems to me that the $64,000 question is what would it have took to give the guys on the ground who have been there for months where you haven't been, what would it have took to get the additional security personnel? Would it take 232, 250 incidences? Would it take a government that had been in power 8 months, not 5 months? What would it have took to do what the professionals in the field felt needed to be done to protect American assets and the lives of these four individuals?

And we will start with you Ambassador, and then Ms. Lamb.

Mr. Kennedy. We do assessments every day of security around the world. We look at every, we look at every location. There were 234 incidents. Only 20 percent of them were in Benghazi, the rest of them were in Tripoli or elsewhere. There had not been a single incident in Benghazi.

Mr. Jordan. Were the more serious ones in Benghazi?

Mr. Kennedy. No, they were elsewhere. There was not ever a single incident in Benghazi of the lethality of the nature of the armed attack which I pointed out was almost unprecedented. Therefore, we then worked very, very carefully. We cannot end the risk to our people overseas. The State Department must go into harm's way. We attempt to mitigate that level of threat. And if we cannot mitigate the level of threat, we will withdraw our people as we have done.

Mr. Jordan. The British ambassador, there was an assassination attempt, our embassy was bombed twice. I guess one of those, what does it take to, again, this is not Congress telling you, these are the professionals in the field who say we need more security personnel in Libya. Okay, maybe all over, this is for Libya, the whole country and you guys say no. And you allude to in your testimony this process of considered judgments of experienced professionals in Washington.

Well, I want to know what those considered judgments of experienced professionals, 234 incidences in the country, violence attacks on our embassy, on Ambassadors, what does it take?

Mr. Kennedy. What I said, Mr. Jordan, there was not any actionable intelligence as the Director of National Intelligence had said----

Mr. Jordan. Are these guys professionals? These guys do their job right? Would you agree with that? These guys said they needed more help.

Mr. Kennedy. If I could finish my statement, sir, please.

Mr. Jordan. Then I want to go to these guys.

Mr. Kennedy. There was no actionable intelligence that was available that indicated----

Mr. Jordan. The word of Mr. Nordstrom and Lieutenant Colonel Wood wasn't good enough?

Mr. Kennedy. There was no actionable intelligence indicating that there was a plan or any indication of a massive attack of the nature and lethality. Yes, absolutely, there was a single rocket-propelled grenade fired at the Red Cross, there was an attack on the British compound. We analyzed those things. And I should also note that, for example, that the French and Italians and the United Nations looked at that same threat stream----

Mr. Jordan. Mr. Nordstrom, do you think they were ever going to give you what you wanted? What do you think would warrant actually them saying you know what, these guys know what they are talking about, we are going to meet their request.

Mr. Nordstrom. Thank you for asking that question.

I actually had that conversation when I came back on leave and for training in February. And I was told by the regional director for Near Eastern Affairs that there had only been one incident involving an American where he was struck by celebratory fire, one of Colonel Wood's employees. The take-away from that for me and my staff, it was abundantly clear we were not going to get resources until the aftermath of an incident. And the question that we would ask is, again, how thin does the ice have to get before someone falls through?

Mr. Jordan. If I could Mr. Chairman, Lieutenant Colonel Wood.

Chairman Issa. The gentleman, Colonel Wood you can answer also.

Colonel Wood. Yes, I agree with Eric Nordstrom. Not only did we have an individual struck by a bullet, but we also had individual members of SST that had a firing shooting incident just before we terminated our duties there.

Again, pointing to the instant ability for anything to happen there, it was an attempted carjacking and there were shots fired going both ways.

Mr. Jordan. If I could, Mr. Chairman, Lieutenant Colonel, Colonel Wood and Mr. Nordstrom, were you pulling your hair out? Were you just flat flabbergasted that, what can we do? What can we say? What can we put in writing? What can we say on the phone? What else can we do? Was that your sense and attitude when you got the answers from Washington that you did?

Colonel Wood. We were fighting a losing battle. We couldn't even keep what we had. We were not even allowed to keep what we had.

Mr. Nordstrom. If I could add to that, and I told the same regional director in a telephone call in Benghazi after he contacted me when I asked for 12 agents. His response to that was you are asking for the sun, moon and the stars. And my response to him, his name is Jim and I said Jim, you know what makes most frustrating about this assignment? It is not the hardships, not the gunfire not the threats; it is dealing and fighting against the people, programs, and personnel who are supposed to be supporting me. And I added it by saying for me, the Taliban is on the inside of the building.

Mr. Jordan. Mr. Chairman, I want to thank our witnesses in particular, Mr. Nordstrom and Colonel Wood for coming forward.

Chairman Issa. I want to thank all our witnesses additionally. In the case of Lieutenant Colonel Wood and Mr. Nordstrom, if as a result perceived or actual of your testimony here today, you are in any way approached or anything happens in your professional lives with the United States Government that you have any questions about, please come to this committee. We take the work of whistleblowers and people who give testimony very seriously.

You have been critical to bring out things that would not have come out of the ordinary course of the administration.

I am going to close only with two comments that I took away from today. One is that you don't reduce security at the same time as you are increasing hazardous duty pay. It doesn't make sense. I haven't heard that question asked and answered, I only heard that it occurred. And I think the State Department should take away from today an understanding that that sends a message that says we will pay you for the risk, we will not pay to have you made safer. That is the impression that anyone would get if you reduce the staffing below recommendations or request and then increase the pay.

I don't think that is what the men and women who serve us overseas want. I know that pay and compensation for hardship is important, but safety comes first especially on these unaccompanied assignments.

Lastly, Colonel Wood, I have a marine fellow that works for me, actually I have a former marine fellow on the side there. The United States military very generously delivers people for other branches for their needs, and in return, those individuals come away understanding and more able to do a broad variety of jobs.

Your time, working with the State Department, is invaluable as you continue your career. I would only say that whether you are talking to your National Guard commanders or the SECDEF or others, that we do appreciate the fact that our men and women have varied careers in which they can assist others with assets that would not be available and then take that back to their units.

And I want to thank you for your service and use you as a conduit for so many men and women who, around the world have added to what otherwise would not be there in the way of security and protection. And with that we stand adjourned.

www.ingramcontent.com/pod-product-compliance
Lightning Source LLC
Chambersburg PA
CBHW070646290526

45790CB00001B/200